Hugh and his team have been instrumental in moving our large family (five Gen 2s and nine Gen 3s) to a very workable succession plan . . . our anxieties of talking about the inevitable and setting a true family plan have been lessened with honest and open discussion led by Hugh's team! Bringing our spouses into the plan has been amazing to watch as they've become vital to creating a happy family succession plan.

JIM BASIL, BASIL FAMILY DEALERSHIPS AND PRESIDENT, JOE BASIL CHEVROLET, BUFFALO, NY

When what matters most is putting in place a plan to allow your successful family business to grow, thrive, and smoothly transition from one generation to the next, while honoring and respecting the talents, needs, and strongest desires of all family members, there's no better strategy than using the expertise and wisdom of a true succession planning professional. Hugh Roberts is the very best at navigating the sometimes treacherous waters to help families achieve their highest objectives for the benefit of their teams and all their loved ones.

LINDA LEITH, PRESIDENT, LEITH AUTOMOTIVE GROUP

For the past decade, Hugh has been more than a trusted adviser—he has been a guiding light for our family and business. This book is a testament to the thorough and thoughtful strategies that he has imparted to us, ensuring that our legacy will not only endure but thrive for generations to come. Hugh's wisdom, dedication, and unwavering support have been instrumental in shaping our path, and we are forever grateful. This is more than a book; it's a road map that reflects the depth of his insight and the profound impact he's had on our lives. Hugh, thank you from the bottom of our hearts for being there every step of the way.

ROLAND SPONGBERG, PRESIDENT & CEO, WKS RESTAURANT GROUP, OWNER OF OVER 300 RESTAURANTS

I0054500

Hugh, I can't thank you enough for your excellent counsel and advice over the last twenty-five-plus years. As you know, when we first started working together, I really didn't feel the urgency to do much estate planning. Part of the reason for that was I didn't have much of an estate. During a lot of this time, I was buying out my partners and wasn't ready to start gifting my estate away. In time, you convinced me of the importance of starting the process and to make progress over time.

As you know, my wife and I have two children. My son worked with me in the business as well as my son-in-law,

About eighteeen months ago, out of nowhere, we made the decision to sell our business after forty-three years. Your planning advice over the years paid us huge dividends when the sale of our business was completed.

Again, I can't thank you enough for staying after me over these last twenty-five-plus years to complete a sound estate plan.

WILLIAM BRADSHAW, FOUNDER, BRADSHAW AUTOMOTIVE GROUP AND PAST PRESIDENT OF THE NATIONAL AUTO DEALERS ASSOCIATION

Family in Business! The words are scary when you hear them or read them. As a lawyer and literary agent, I have had the privilege and burden for the past thirty years of having two of my adult children working alongside me and the joy of having them become my partners. Hugh Roberts and his partner, Jeff Bannon, stepped into the world of our business and helped save not only our business but our family as well, for which I will be eternally grateful. The principles and counsel Hugh has so eloquently described in *Help! I've Got Family in the Business* will provide you with a great start on the kind of results my sons and I found by listening carefully to and acting upon Hugh's wisdom. What Hugh says in this book really works! It is a read that is more than worth your investment.

SEALY YATES, SENIOR PARTNER, YATES & YATES

Hugh Roberts has been a huge influence in growing our family business and planning to pass it on to the next generation. He has helped our sons' development toward a true working partnership, business planning to lead our growth, and long-term wealth planning for our entire family. I consider him an asset and a true trusted friend!

TOM GILL, OWNER, TOM GILL CHEVROLET

Navigating the balance between family and business is incredibly challenging. Hugh, someone I've had the privilege to know, has a unique talent for helping families work through these challenges with wisdom and care.

In *Help! I've Got Family in the Business*, Hugh shares his years of experience in a way that's easy to understand and incredibly valuable for anyone dealing with the complexities of a family business. He covers everything from generational struggles to estate planning mistakes, offering real advice that's helped many families find success and harmony.

I've watched in awe as Hugh masterfully navigated our own family through difficult conversations and complex issues. Thanks to his guidance, we were able to find solutions that were fair, sustainable, and beneficial for everyone involved. If your family or business is fortunate enough to work with Hugh, consider it a true gift. And if you're seeking guidance on how to manage or prevent the inevitable time bombs that come with mixing family and business, this book is your road map. I'm grateful that Hugh has shared his wealth of knowledge in writing, ensuring that more families can benefit from his expertise. This book is not just a guide; it's a lifeline for those committed to preserving both their family relationships and their business legacies.

BETH BEANS GILBERT, VP, FRED BEANS AUTOMOTIVE GROUP

# HELP!

## I've Got Family In The Business

**10 Time Bombs That Blow Up Family Business**

# Hugh B. Roberts CFP® CSP®

bookVillages

*Help! I've Got Family in the Business:*
  *10 Time Bombs That Blow Up Family Business*

© 2024 Hugh B. Roberts

All rights reserved. No part of this publication may be reproduced in any form without written permission from Book Villages, P.O. Box 64526, Colorado Springs, CO 80962. www.bookvillages.com

All Scripture quotations are taken from the Holy Bible, New International Version®, NIV® Copyright ©1973, 1978, 1984, 2011 by Biblica, Inc.® Used by permission. All rights reserved worldwide.

Paperback ISBN: 978-1-95756-633-7

Cover Design by Michael-Paul Terranova
Interior Design by Niddy Griddy Design, Inc.

LCCN: 2024925228

Printed in the United States of America

1 2 3 4 5 6 7 8 9 10 Printing/Year 28 27 26 25 24

*To my wife, Lisa, and our wonderful family for your love, support, and encouragement.*

*To my partners and colleagues at The Rawls Group, who inspire me daily with your dedication to helping our business owner clients perpetuate their family business legacies.*

*To the business owner clients and their families with whom I've had the privilege of working.*

*To Meg Snow, my executive assistant of thirty-two years, who always has my back.*

*To my son-in-law, Michael Paul Terranova, for your graphic artist creativity and talent displayed in the cartoons and cover of this book.*

*To Sealy Yates and Mike Salisbury of Yates & Yates, who provided guidance and direction in the development and publishing of this book.*

*To Karen Pickering and her outstanding team at Book Villages for your support and knowledge needed to publish this book.*

# CONTENTS

# FOREWORD

I am honored as a first-generation automobile dealer to have the opportunity to write the Foreword to Hugh Roberts book *"Help! I've Got Family in the Business."*

I started as a single entrepreneur at the age of twenty by purchasing a service station repair shop in Yardley, PA. I began with one employee and myself and grew that business over twelve years. I knew all along that I wanted to be an automobile dealer. I worked hard to save money and looked for opportunities.

In 1972, I joined Bill Marsh as a partner at his Ford dealership in Newtown, PA. In 1975 I came to Doylestown, PA and purchased a Ford dealership. Today we own twenty-seven automobile dealerships, six collision centers and the largest parts distribution centers in the United States employing over 360 employees. Today our company has over 2,000 employees.

In 1997, we began to address estate planning steps designed to minimize taxes and position our business for succession. In 2018 my attorney and CPA advised that we needed additional help to achieve my goal of continuing my family business legacy. We interviewed three different companies and decided to partner with Hugh Roberts and his team. Hugh and his team have done remarkable things to bring our family business together. They helped us find a way to have our company continue into the second and third generation. My daughter and son-in-law are actively involved in our business on a daily basis. I've had the pleasure of enjoying my grandson enter the business as well. We managed to do all of this through Hugh Roberts and his team. They helped us strategize a plan to bring a family member into our business. To support my grandson's growth, we've set up three team members to assist in his growth in this industry. We did not allow this until he had three years of other outside experience.

Hugh and his team have helped us set a course that I believe will give us the opportunity to continue our business into the third generation and continue to grow it.

Many family businesses know the frustrations—especially with family members in the business. I have experienced my own frustrations as the founder. Over the last six years, Hugh and his team have helped us establish a plan for the future. He's worked with us to develop a Board of Directors and develop leadership teams to support our future growth. This has been accomplished through careful planning and regular meetings with Hugh and his team.

Hugh also has been a tremendous help in our Estate Planning. I wish we had started this sooner because there's an advantage in a company that has a founder because there's another generation of compounding that takes place. I personally missed a good strategy for planning for the future. However, Hugh and the team helped us establish this.

I've had the opportunity to read Hugh's book and fully recommend it to anyone who has or is involved in their family business. It will assist you in establishing a plan for the future along with the growth and continuity of working together as well as having the ability to correct the mistakes made along the way, while still being able to celebrate the good times .

Fred Beans
Founder, Fred Beans Automotive Group

# INTRODUCTION

If the title *Help! I've Got Family in the Business* caught your eye, it's likely you are facing challenges working with family members in your business. *Frustrating* is probably a mild term for the emotions you've experienced. You wonder if anyone understands your situation. "Am I the only one dealing with these kinds of problems? Are there any answers? I love my family, but they're driving me crazy!"

You might be thinking, "This business has provided a wonderful lifestyle for our family for decades, but if we don't find some better solutions to the problems we're facing, we'll have to sell. And selling is the last thing I want to do. Can anyone help us achieve our goal of business success and family harmony?"

Your dream may be to see your children succeed in your business and continue the family legacy, but the challenges of mixing family and business can turn your dreams into nightmares. What are the secrets to win-win solutions for parents and their children to achieve Succession Success™?

Your situation is real; it's usually emotional, and you want answers now. "Ours can't be the only family business struggling to make it work. I'd like to learn from others, avoiding mistakes if possible."

I've had the privilege of working with family business owners and their families nationwide for over forty years. Through their stories I will attempt to illuminate mistakes made, problems and consequences overcome, and, most importantly, how Succession Success™ was achieved. Instead of avoiding these nightmare issues, you'll see how family harmony and your legacy dream are attainable.

As much as you may feel your situation is unique, there are likely many other families experiencing similar challenges. That's the good news, because others have gone before you and have found answers where they didn't expect to find any. Hope is powerful; if you don't have hope, find someone who believes in you and lean into their hope until you find your own.

These family business succession stories are challenging and often keep you up at night. It's easy to rationalize problems, hoping somehow they will go away. But like most problems, if not addressed, they usually just get bigger. I trust that this book will provide you with hope and the courage to seek help.

**Bottom line: I want to help you promote family harmony while achieving business success.**

Knowing how important it is to maintain confidentiality with my clients, I've altered stories to protect the privacy of those involved, while maintaining the genuine real-life impact. However, in my experience, family business issues are universal. While there is a significant possibility my readers will interpret a reference as being about them, the story may, in fact, be about many, many families. My hope is that you will be able to relate to these stories about real-life families involved in their family businesses and find commonality that helps you address your own family business issues. Bottom line: I want to help you promote family harmony while achieving business success.

It is also important to note that over the four decades I've been working with family business owners, some of the most successful have been women but most have been men. The stories in this book often reflect male owners. Fortunately, many of these family businesses now have daughters and granddaughters who are taking over as the successors. It is clear that slowly but surely the work barriers are being broken down by highly competent, committed women leaders who have proven their ability to succeed in the often male-dominated workplace.

Undoubtedly, these women owners view some of the family business time bombs differently and will find ways to defuse the bombs the male-dominated workplace neglected. Nevertheless, families are complex, and whether companies are led by a male or a female, family business owners are likely to be challenged to succeed as businesses involving family members.

I'm happily married, the father of two wonderful married children in their forties, and a grandfather to five special girls, ranging in age from five to seventeen, so I can relate to many family challenges. I often say, "I do a great job talking to someone else's child. It's a whole different ball game when talking with your own—and mine are great people." We all know there is more at stake when addressing your own family members. When addressing issues of family in business together, I can fully appreciate the joy and the pain that come with being involved in family relationships.

For the past four decades as a family business succession planner, I've worked exclusively with hundreds of family business owners of capital-intensive, complex businesses in many, many sectors—automotive dealers, manufacturers, distributors, real estate developers, general contractors and subcontractors, multi-franchise food distributors, to name a few. I've been a partner with The Rawls Group for twenty-two years, whose exclusive commitment to succession planning with family-owned businesses

**What do all our clients have in common?** *Family, with all of the good, the bad, and the ugly that comes with being in business with your relatives. So, let's examine why family business can be so challenging and rewarding at the same time.*

now spans fifty-one years, involving thousands of family businesses nationwide. What do all our clients have in common? *Family*, with all of the good, the bad, and the ugly that comes with being in business with your relatives. So, let's examine why family business can be so challenging and rewarding at the same time.

# Dream or Nightmare?

"What do you mean you're not coming into
the family business?!?"

# DREAM OR NIGHTMARE?

*"That's not fair—what about me?"*

*"My father won't retire—and I'm in my fifties. When do I get my chance?"*

*"That's not fair. . . . My brother expects me to do all the work while he gets equal pay."*

*"My parents expect me to run the business for the sake of the whole family. This is a father-son business, but my siblings think it is a family business."*

*"My children want to push me out. I built the business, not them."*

*"Why won't my daughter run the business the way I did?"*

*"I need Dad's help, but he never has time for me!"*

*"Why can't my children appreciate what I've done for them?"*

*"Why won't my children work as hard as I did?"*

*"I have three children—how do I pick my successor?"*

*"Generational differences are driving me crazy!"*

*"They're my family, but I'm tired of carrying them."*

*"Will my key managers ever respect my kids?"*

*"My kids aren't meeting my expectations."*

*"The business is splitting our family apart—what do we do?"*

Sound familiar? Is your dream of continuing the family business legacy becoming a nightmare?

*Succession* was your dream, possibly from the day your son or daughter came into this world. "To watch my son succeed in my business is the greatest joy of my life!" exclaimed my auto dealer client. You may not have been so bold, because you didn't want to force the business onto your kid, but deep down it seemed like a dream that would hopefully one day come true.

**Is your dream of continuing the family business legacy becoming a nightmare?**

Recently, a Generation 2 business owner client expressed his goal was to achieve a multi-generational family business legacy. *"That's what I'm talking about!"* How proud you'd feel to have your son/daughter/grandson/granddaughter follow in your footsteps, committing their life to carrying on your life's work.

This week I met with Generations 3, 4, and 5 as they planned how to continue their distributorship family business legacy, which has been sustained for over 110 years! That's impressive, and they take succession very seriously. But, imagine the pressure to make sure the business continues!

"Someday, we're going to do this together—my child and I working side by side, growing our family business." What a thrill for the business owner to see their offspring wanting to emulate them, learn from them, spend time together, and create this magnificent company that positively impacts their community. It's a dream come true!

Family businesses come into being because entrepreneurs like you had a dream and were willing to "put it all on red"—risking everything. Simply put, most family businesses started with the owner committing all he or she had financially to go into business for themselves. I've heard countless stories from my business owner clients who saved and saved and saved and then risked it all,

> "How can I keep this wonderful business going after I'm gone?"

even taking on significant debt, just to have the opportunity to go into business for themself. To be your own boss, to have control over your own destiny, to reap the rewards for your hard work, creativity, and commitment—that's how family businesses get started. I always love hearing business owners share how they got started, because each story is unique and demonstrates the pioneer spirit that makes our country great.

When you've committed heart and soul, blood, sweat, and tears, and every penny you've got to making your business dream come true, eventually you start to think, "How can I keep this wonderful business going after I'm gone?" *Succession* is now important to you!

*What went wrong? Why do you need help?* Families are the best of times and can be the worst of times, and when you put family and business in the same test tube, sometimes the chemistry creates explosions.

All families are a little dysfunctional, and that's what makes it challenging to mix families and business together. Let's face it, it would be crazy to run a business like a family, and you certainly cannot manage a family like a business. "Family business" is an oxymoron. *Family* is supposed to be about unconditional love and acceptance—"I love you just because"—while *business* is about conditional performance— "What have you done for me lately?" Striking the right balance between being focused on what is best for your family versus what is best for your business is usually challenging and sometimes just plain difficult.

> *Family* is supposed to be about unconditional love and acceptance — "I love you just because" —while *business* is about conditional performance — "What have you done for me lately?"

When your son or daughter first joined you in your business, it was a wonderful day. "I thought this was the start of something great," said the owner of a manufacturing company. "My son had gotten an excellent education with an MBA, and now he and I were going to work together, growing our business and having fun. This was my dream come true!" But "then it began to fall apart—he didn't want to do the things he needed to do to learn the business. He thought he didn't need to do those things. He thought he knew everything since obviously he had an MBA. He came and went when he felt like it, and unfortunately, I didn't hold him accountable. I had experienced problems with my siblings, and I didn't want to risk losing my relationship with my son. My dream became a nightmare!" Several years later he sold his company, and his dream went down the drain.

You have your own story, and hopefully the final chapter has not yet been written. You are looking for answers to fulfill your dream of a family business succession legacy. There are a host of potential minefields you have to navigate. So, let's examine **10 Time Bombs That Blow Up Family Business**.

# 1

# Generational Differences

"Dad says he's open to new ideas...But."

# Time Bomb #1

# *Struggles Between Generations*

## "IT'S TOUGH BEING YOUR KID"

"It must be tough being your kid," I said to Julius Erving as we waited to get our luggage at LAX several years ago. He looked at me with a frown that seemed to say, "What do you mean? (I'm a good guy.)" I responded, "Because there is only one Dr. J! You cast a giant shadow; that must be pretty challenging for your children." There was nothing disparaging about my comment. I was simply stating the fact that with every successful person, their children face the often insurmountable challenge of reaching the same pinnacle of success. You don't have to be a famous personality for that statement to be true. The same is definitely true for my business owner clients.

**For many children of business owners, living in your shadow is daunting or, in some cases, a competition they cannot win.**

As business owners of multimillion-dollar companies, with your net worth in the top 1 percent (or even smaller) of all Americans, you represent achievement. You are leaders in your community, highly respected, lords of your universe. Congratulations!

> "You have a Ted Williams complex. He was the last .400 hitter in Major League Baseball, and you expect your son to be a .400 hitter in your business, just like you are."

While this is all highly commendable and represents a lifetime of excellence, for many children of business owners, living in your shadow is daunting or, in some cases, a competition they cannot win. Unfortunately, all too often my partners at The Rawls Group and I are tasked with helping business owner families address the family and business challenges created by mismatched expectations between the owner and his children.

After listening to my auto dealer client use highly derogatory terms to describe his son, which seemed to suggest his son wasn't performing in the business to the standards his father had set, I said to the dealer, "You have a Ted Williams complex." (He was a Greatest Generation auto dealer.) "What do you mean?" he asked. "Well, Ted Williams was the last .400 hitter in Major League Baseball, and you expect your son to be a .400 hitter in your business, just like you are."

The truth was, his son had a sterling record as GM of one of their most profitable stores, absolutely knocking the cover off the ball profitwise, making $5 million-plus net. But his father was GM of their most profitable store and was making just a little bit more profit than his son's store, though arguably in a much better market.

"My son should be doing $6 to $7 million in his store—if he

just worked harder!" I knew that Dad did nothing but work, so I said, "What if your son doesn't want to work twenty-four seven like you do?" "Well, he's not going to play on my team," exclaimed the dealer. "Sounds to me like you are the only one not willing to give your son credit for the great job he is doing," I responded.

Fortunately, we continued to work together for almost ten years until he died, and I hope I was able to help this father/dealer gain some perspective. As a father, I know all too well how much my expectations for my children can become challenges to their growth and development.

John (not his real name) owned a large construction company, employing hundreds of people. Beginning our initial analysis of a business's succession planning environment, we routinely interview selected key managers and include questions regarding the son's or daughter's potential to someday succeed their father or mother. Unanimously, the managers replied that his daughter was an excellent leader and would do a great job leading the company. When we shared this with John, his reply was, "They're wrong!"

> **Unanimously, the managers replied that his daughter was an excellent leader and would do a great job leading the company. When we shared this with John, his reply was, "They're wrong!"**

John is a "my way or the highway" type leader, and his processes and procedures are the only way. His daughter is relationally focused and uses her ability to motivate her team to drive profits. But to her father, "If you don't do it my way, then you're wrong!" My response to Dad was, "Of course, her leadership style will be different from yours, but is she getting the results (assuming she is ethically and legally in alignment with your business practices)?"

The next generation will do things differently than you did and often more effectively.

Growing up, who did you measure yourself against to determine how you were doing in life? I'll bet it was your parents and siblings. This can be especially challenging for children of highly successful parents like our business owner clients.

> As a 1 percenter financially, our business owner clients are in the "Financial Hall of Fame." That can feel like climbing Mount Everest to your child, who is trying to emulate your success.

As parents, we clearly want to help our children succeed, knowing we have set the bar very high. For my business partner Jeff Bannon, who was a professional baseball player, if his son makes the high school or college team, that will be nice, but it will be nothing close to what he had accomplished. To make my point, it is interesting to note that there are zero father/son combinations in the Major League Baseball Hall of Fame. As a 1 percenter financially, our business owner clients are in the "Financial Hall of Fame." That can feel like climbing Mount Everest to your child, who is trying to emulate your success.

Assuming your child wants to follow in your footsteps and get involved in your business, he/she is motivated. So how do you mentor your child and give them the greatest possibilities for succeeding? First, you probably know that your child may be very different from you, personality-wise. So, if your child feels they must be like you to succeed, they are likely doomed to failure.

A couple years ago, I met with a business owner for the first time who began telling me his sad story, involving his son who had always wanted to follow in his footsteps but suddenly changed his mind in college and decided to become a doctor. The business owner said he wanted to be supportive of his son's decision but was also disappointed, as his son's decision was a complete shock. He told me his son had worked during the summer in the sales department and turned out to be an abysmal failure. Immediately his son switched to premed.

I asked the dealer if he and his son had talked about this, and he said they hadn't. "What's wrong with being a doctor? I shouldn't complain," he said. I agreed that being a doctor is a highly commendable ambition, but I said, "Did it ever occur to you that you are a fabulous salesman, and your son likely came to the conclusion that he couldn't be a dealer because he believes he has to be like you? When comparing himself to you, he may easily have thought, "This business isn't for me," because he had no other perspective."

**They don't have to be like you!**

Those of us who have been around family-owned businesses for many years know that many owners are not natural salesmen, so instead they hire salespeople, while they lead their companies through maximizing their skill sets. Only you can help your children understand that they can be successful if they have the drive, commitment, work ethic, desire to learn, and positive attitude—and *they don't have to be like you!*

## "MY KID DOESN'T WORK AS HARD AS I DO"

You only know one way to work—*hard!* Your work is your life, and you believe the saying, "The harder I work, the luckier I get." To you, work means bell to bell, early mornings and late nights, weekends—work, work, work! Work gives you purpose and meaning, and since you own the company, you are thinking about work twenty-four seven. The daughter of one of my clients, who is a leader in her family business, expressed, "There was no work-life balance in our household—family dinner was another business meeting."

The underlying feeling is that if you are going to succeed in your business, you must put in the hours. Dad feels there are too many things and people to do the job on part-time hours (defined as twelve-hour days). Besides, it sets a bad example if the boss isn't "working hard" (defined as being on the job around the clock).

> "I'm at the office every Saturday— why doesn't my son work at least some Saturdays? I know he wants time with his children, but we've got a business to run!"

"I'm at the office every Saturday— why doesn't my son work at least some Saturdays? I know he wants time with his children, but we've got a business to run!" Bottom line: Dad feels if he does not stay involved and in control, the business will suffer profitwise. This creates a fear that often freezes Dad from turning over management authority or transferring stock, especially if it involves control of the business.

For some owners, involvement means they come to work every day, even though they are in their seventies or eighties. There is a problem if Dad is unwilling to relinquish authority or must be involved in everything. Unless job descriptions and lines of authority are carefully communicated among Dad, his son or daughter, and all the employees, his son or daughter may never be able to take charge and develop into Dad's successor as long as Dad is "on the job."

Some of this is due to habits—when the business was small, Dad had to be involved in everything because his team was small. "I did what I had to do." But now the business has grown substantially, and often we see the next generation is better at delegating. One daughter said, "I work smarter, and Dad works harder." Dad unfortunately only knows one way. This reminds me of a book I read years ago: *When I Relax I Feel Guilty* by Tim Hansel. The result is Dad continues to stay involved in all aspects of his business and resents his children's work ethic—"My kids are unwilling to put in the effort."

"I don't have confidence my kid can run the business," exclaimed the seventy-two-year-old owner. I'd love to have a dollar for every time I've heard that expressed. Unfortunately, it is often directed at a highly effective son or daughter who is organized, structured, and strategic and commands the respect of the management team but frustrates Dad because he/she doesn't work bell to bell.

> **"I'm waiting to see if my son/daughter will step up to the challenge. I'm not sure they are willing to do what is necessary."**

When you are frustrated and don't have confidence that your kid will be effective running your business, what do you do? Usually, *nothing*! Often this is an excuse for Dad to keep on working to "protect my business." But it also means you're not likely to relinquish leadership, authority, or control. Owners who want their business to continue after they're gone know that transition needs to happen *but* often do nothing to prepare the way. "I'm waiting to see if my son/daughter will step up to the challenge. I'm not sure they are willing to do what is necessary." Behind these statements is fear that if they don't work "the way I did," the business will fail.

Clearly, your son or daughter must perform and must be effective. This productivity demands they do the job, exercising leadership that drives their management team to profitably run the business. *But* they don't have to do it the way you did.

# GENERATIONAL DIFFERENCES = CONFLICT

"I flew in an airplane for the first time when I was nineteen, my son when he was nineteen months." And you can imagine how different the worldview is of my client's daughter, who has never flown commercially (they've always owned a jet during her lifetime).

We are all impacted by the world we grew up in and live in now. So, it's no surprise that communication in a family-owned business between different generations can be challenging at times. All too often, conflict and friction are the inevitable result. Most of the businesses my partners and I work with involve at least two generations and often three. So, strap on your Kevlar jacket—let's talk about our differences!

I've been to many business owner meetings, usually held at beautiful resorts. Here's a typical conversation I heard a few years ago between a father and his son:

"Son, I want to share a few things about how I was successful. First, no debt—debt is a killer. Make sure you stay out of debt!"

"But, Dad, in my MBA program they told me it's all about OPM—other people's money. That's how you get ahead, by using debt leverage."

"Well, all I know, son, is that you have to watch every dollar, so I fly coach, but you, you're the big shot flying first class."

"Dad, what do you do on a plane?"

"Usually, I read or take a nap."

"Precisely—I work on planes. Have you ever tried to open a laptop in coach? Oh, I forgot, you don't use a laptop!"

"Well, son, I love it when you talk about work, because that's what my generation does. We work—days, nights, weekends, whatever it takes."

"Yes, Dad, that's all you do, and my siblings and I never saw you. I'm not about to do that to my family!"

"Well, son, let's get back to expenses. I have no problem staying at the Holiday Inn, but you're the big shot staying at the Ritz. Why is that?"

"Because we're rich, Dad!"

"No, son, I'm rich—you're not!"

No wonder older generations can get cranky when dealing with their children, and the children get frustrated with their parents—both obviously seeing the world through a different lens.

I remember speaking with a Greatest Generation owner of a highly complex multi-business operation, and I asked him, "Help me understand—your son flies in your corporate jet, and you fly coach. Why?" He looked at me like I was stupid and replied, "Because it's cheaper!"

When his son later paid a huge price acquiring a new business, this father called me in a state of panic and said he wanted to buy a big life insurance policy on his son. "My son must be crazy paying that kind of money. If something happens to him, I don't want to get stuck paying off that debt." To be noted, this son is a fantastic businessman who grew the family business substantially, but his father always saw him as being a bit reckless.

Perspectives are definitely different:

| Greatest Generation (GG) | Baby Boomers | Gen X/Millennials |
|---|---|---|
| "Waste not, want not" | "Image is everything." | "Work/Life balance" |
| "My kid spends too much." | "Customers expect us to look successful." | "Me first" |

When I first started in the succession planning business in the 1980s, you often walked into the office of a Greatest Generation business owner and saw old carpet, a worn-out chair, etc. His children, in contrast, are more likely to want "new and expensive." The GG grew up in a world where credit was unusual and everyone had less. His children grew up with wealth all around them. Advertising focused everyone on wanting and buying things now, not later.

| Greatest Generation (GG) | Younger Generations |
| --- | --- |
| "If you have enough cash, buy it. If not, wait." | "Instant credit—buy now" "Earn to spend" |
| "Delay gratification" | "Immediate gratification" |
| "Don't go into debt—you could lose it all." | "Debt is just a part of doing business." |

The GG lived through the Depression and have a constant fear of losing it all. A GG sees his children's willingness to incur debt as irresponsible use of money. The GG saves and loves to see his bank and investment balances growing while his children wonder, "When are we going to be able to enjoy any of the fruits of our success?"

> **The GG lived through the Depression and have a constant fear of losing it all.**

Watching the bottom line and expenses often categorizes the GG's approach. Fear of losing it all, coupled with the concerns of growing older (no time to recover if I lose money), often causes conflict with his children, who want to grow and expand.

Fathers need to remember their entrepreneurial spirit when they were young and wanting to make it happen. Many children do not want to be caretakers of the family fortune; instead, they want to grow the business and make their mark—and that involves debt and risk.

| Grandfather | Dad | Child |
|---|---|---|
| "The harder you work, the luckier you get!" | "Dad did nothing but work." | "I need balance in my life." |
| "I worked night and day to provide for my family." | "I need to spend time with my family." | "I can use digital skills to work smarter." |

Again, the world we live in is different. There is a greater emphasis on spending time with our families. In the GG's era, he went to work, and Mom was at home taking care of the family. Today, both parents are usually working, and parents are often shouldering the "home and family" responsibilities together. Generational differences often cause older parents to be frustrated by their children's work ethic, but they will compliment their children for being great parents. Younger generations value work-life balance above just making money.

**What is the American Dream?**

What is the American Dream? To give our families a better life—a larger home in a better neighborhood, more education, more of life's experiences, more security. "I started out with nothing." For many business owners, that is exactly correct, but your children grew up in the wealth environment you created for them. Today, ironically, your children are members of a generation that will *not* do as well financially as their parents did.

"Walk a mile in my shoes," says the old song. Unfortunately, that is hard to do! It helps to recognize our children, parents, and grandparents grew up in a different environment than we did. Therefore, we are going to see and value things differently.

> "That's right, Dad. You had it easy. You started at the bottom—you had nowhere to go but up. Everything you did was a success. My brothers and I had to start at the top."

Each viewpoint has strengths and weaknesses. For example, working hard is good—but working too hard can create problems at home. Careful management of money is good—but all too often the fear of spoiling your children causes resentment, especially if you raised them in a lifestyle they are unable to emulate.

"I don't have a house at the beach," said the exasperated father, reflecting on his kids buying a second home. "But you could own a dozen houses and spend more time enjoying your success with us, instead of working all the time" came the frustrated reply from his daughter.

Taking time to understand our differences and appreciate that other generations have wisdom—regardless of their age, older or younger—will help alleviate some of the tension created by our generational differences. You may be surprised—it's possible your kids, parents, or even grandparents might know something you could learn from.

## LIVING IN DAD'S SHADOW

"You don't understand, Dad. You had it easy," exclaimed the business owner's daughter.

"Easy! Are you kidding me? I grew up on the wrong side of the tracks with an alcoholic father who died when I was twelve. I started with nothing and had to earn every penny. This business was built with my blood, sweat, and tears! What are you talking about—easy?!"

"That's right, Dad. You had it easy. You started at the bottom—you had nowhere to go but up. Everything you did was a success. My brothers and I had to start at the top."

This statement reflected great insight on the daughter's part, and every successful business owner needs to remember this when trying to understand what makes your children tick. Your children face a daunting task trying to put their own mark on this world, especially since you are the king of your business empire, in which they are trying to excel.

It's your world your children are entering when they begin working in your business. If you want them to succeed you someday and continue your family business legacy, you need to understand the challenges they face—starting with you.

"I love coming to work every day!" exclaimed the eighty-one-year-old business owner. No doubt, and he still had plenty of gas left in his tank. Energetic and mentally sharp, his idea of "retirement" was to come in to work at 10 a.m. ("But I stay at least until 5 p.m.") As the founder of his business empire, he was extremely proud of what he had accomplished and felt he was still able to contribute. So, what's the problem?

> "Will your son/daughter be ready when the time comes?" and "Is your involvement sabotaging your succession plans?"

If you don't make room for your successor(s) to grow in their levels of leadership, they never will. Are you dominating the landscape, or are you creating an environment where they can succeed you (assuming they're committed, qualified, and have earned the respect of the management team)?

I have seen successful transitions between generations, but also disasters for the business and the family. The questions that need to be addressed are, "Will your son/daughter be ready when the time comes?" and "Is your involvement sabotaging your succession plans?"

Frequently, the first answer is "No" or, at best, "The transition would not be smooth." The decisions you make about your involvement will impact the successful transition of your business.

> One business owner told me, "I know who I am, and unless I get out of the way, everyone would continue to look to me, and my kids would never get the chance to become the leaders I want them to be."

So, what needs to happen for your legacy to continue successfully?

First, as the patriarch or matriarch, you must realize you cast a very long shadow. It is often extremely difficult as your son or daughter to be viewed against your success. Undoubtedly you are a strong personality, and you have been extremely successful, making it difficult for your child to measure up to your accomplishments.

Depending on your personality and management style, you may need to change things to give your son or daughter the opportunity to make the necessary decisions to prepare them to be able to run your business. If you are a dominating personality or have a strong need to control, you need to look in the mirror and convince yourself to back off and give your son or daughter some space—or your succession dream will one day become a nightmare.

One business owner told me, "I know who I am, and unless

I get out of the way, everyone would continue to look to me, and my kids would never get the chance to become the leaders I want them to be." So, he lives in Florida six months of the year. He stays in regular contact with his son and daughter who are running the company, but managers look first to his children for leadership.

Moving out of state has definitely helped in their situation, but there is one huge pitfall you must avoid if you go this route. All too often, fathers exercise "seagull management"—they fly in, poop all over everything, and fly out! In other words, you can't expect to show up every now and then and overturn major decisions that have been made. This is a recipe for business and family disaster.

Allowing your successor children to do things differently is tough on the older generation, but it is important to their learning cycle, especially when they make mistakes. That's how you learned.

Are you still demanding that your children do things your way, regardless of how long they have worked in your business? It is one thing to train your child to be successful when they are in their twenties or thirties. It is quite a different thing to still be expecting significant change to happen when your child is in his/her forties and fifties.

By continuing to badger them to change at this point, you are only damaging your relationship, and change is not likely to happen. I told one seventy-year-old business owner, "Your son is forty-six. The die is cast. He is obviously his own man and wants to do things differently from the way you do things." This son was a very accomplished executive, and he definitely did things differently than his father.

In contrast to the frustration the above business owner and his son were experiencing, I work with an owner in his seventies who is addressing this issue in a very satisfying and effective manner. George (not his real name) recognizes that his son is not the gregarious salesman and motivational leader he is. The son, Jason (not his real name), is solid financially, good on administrative details, presents himself well with the public and manufacturers, and has good business sense. Therefore, George and Jason decided the best approach was to hire a COO who could manage day-to-day operations and keep the troops fired up and selling. George continues to be involved, but he is conscious about sharing the spotlight and deferring decision-making to his son and the COO.

Due in large part to the father's sensitivity to his own dominant personality and his willingness to back off, his son welcomes Dad's involvement and continued expert advice. Most importantly, their relationship as father and son remains strong.

Expectations are extremely important and must be clearly stated and defined between an owner and his/her children operating together in the family business. With the help of a trained succession planner, you need to define and get on paper what each of you expects of the other in terms of decision-making authority, time spent on the job, who is responsible for what areas, profitability benchmarks, etc.

Clearly defined expectations, agreed upon by both parties in writing, will make it more likely that business owner parents and their children can coexist positively and effectively, both for the betterment of the business and your family. Hopefully you, too, can echo the words of one business owner: "Having my father involved with me in our business is wonderful!" Obviously, she is no longer living in Dad's shadow.

# 2

# Entitlement
# The Kiss of Death

"Being the boss' kid is great."

# Time Bomb #2

# Are You the Problem?

## ARE YOU MAKING EXCUSES FOR YOUR FAMILY?

Tough as nails when making business decisions *but* soft as butter when holding your kids accountable—is that you? I see it all the time working with the owners of multimillion-dollar family businesses. Your vision is to have your family join you and continue your family business legacy. What a wonderful dream . . . until reality pops your balloon. What happens? All too often your child doesn't measure up, but you want them to succeed so badly that you are willing to overlook and minimize their actions, something you wouldn't accept from any other employee.

**Tough as nails when making business decisions but soft as butter when holding your kids accountable—is that you?**

Unfortunately, all too often business owners make different

decisions regarding their family than they'd make for anyone else, excusing the behavior of their children. For over fifty years my partners and I at The Rawls Group have watched highly successful, strong business leaders, with a history of making the difficult decisions demanded of business owners, compromise their values when making decisions regarding family members. *Why?*

It's simple—decisions regarding your family members affect Thanksgiving! Most of us want to enjoy time with our family members, and Thanksgiving is a perfect example of when we want our family to be harmonious. Yours is a *family business*, and if you make decisions regarding family members that upset family dynamics, you pay a price—one that business owners often are unwilling to pay.

> **Decisions regarding your family members affect Thanksgiving!**

I recently met with a business owner whose niece wants to get hired into the family business. So, what's the problem? She's been fired from her current job and needs the family business to rescue her. If this were not a family member, no further discussion would be needed—this person would not get hired. But, because she is family, we are still talking about how to make it happen. Why? Because the owner is afraid of her parents' reaction and the repercussions within the family. "You hired your daughter; why won't you hire my daughter?" And we all know how protective and defensive parents can get regarding their children!

"Put my child on a fast track" was the instruction I was given for an owner's child. *Why?* Because in a short time the owner wanted his child ready, so he could back off and be less involved in day-to-day operations. The owner's timetable for semi-retirement was dictating the successor's development time frame. Clearly, every child is different, and some children have the aptitude and attitude to move fast in their development. But is the time frame related to the parent's objective, or are we adequately preparing the child to be a successful successor? I see this as an excuse for not making the right call regarding preparing your successor.

"Why are you paying all three of your children the same?" was a question I directed to a business owner. The children were not contributing at the same level, and their responsibilities were definitely disparate. Not only that, but one child was performing at a much higher level than the other siblings. "Because their mother wants to make sure we treat all three the same" was the response.

> "Why are you paying all three of your children the same?"

This rationalizing of decisions to prevent family disharmony is an excuse for not making prudent business decisions. "You *aren't* treating them equally—you are not adequately rewarding the one who is most productive, and you are over-rewarding the one who is least productive," I responded. Unfortunately, rarely does each of your children contribute at the same level as their siblings. By paying them all the same, aren't you just excusing the behaviors of the least productive and not rewarding your productive child?

The same applies to transferring the stock in your business equally to all your children. I often hear, "We want to be fair to all our children" or "We love all our children the same, so we don't want to treat any of them differently" (for fear that a child will feel unloved or unappreciated). This is just an excuse for not making the tough decisions that are demanded of successful business owners. If one of your children is carrying the load, then he/she needs to be rewarded.

"I don't want my child to have to do all the demeaning things I had to do when I was new in the business," replied one business owner. He wanted to insulate his child from the difficult path that he had walked, starting at the bottom and working his way up the ladder. Sure, it was tough and there were lots of things you did that you hated, but that's what built into you the toughness that helped you succeed. It allowed you to understand what each of your employees deals with, creating an understanding of how tough your business can be.

It's hard being the bad guy, requiring your child to pay his/her dues, but that's what creates effective leaders. Otherwise, you are excusing them from the very real learning experiences that will create effective, productive successors. Don't deprive your child of the required tough experiences that will shape them as a leader.

I'm a father of two and a grandfather of five—I understand how hard it is to see your children struggle, and there is a huge part of me that wants to insulate them from harm emotionally or physically. But we all know that life is tough—and your business is tough—and if they are going to be ready, willing, and able to succeed in life and your business, then you can't make excuses. You have to treat them as you would any employee—demanding that they perform at their highest level.

Will they be ready to take over when you're gone? That depends on whether you make excuses and give them the easy route. Do you care enough to prepare them by demanding they work their butt off (like you did) and bring a can-do attitude to work every day?

## ENTITLEMENT: THE KISS OF DEATH

*"It's not my fault my parents are wealthy!"*
*"But we always get demo cars!"*
*"What do you mean I can't take two weeks off to go to Europe—all my friends are going!"*
*"I know I need to come to work on time, but . . ."*
*"I have an attendance problem."*

Just when I think I've heard it all, the excuses keep on coming, and unfortunately, all too many business owners just throw up their hands, in effect saying, "What can I do about it?"

"I don't have to do it. I'm the owner's son!" exclaimed the newest employee of the family business. For his father, this was the start of a long-term nightmare. The owner's dream of seeing his son succeed him looked to

**"I don't have to do it. I'm the owner's son!"**

be "dreaming the impossible dream." How does this happen, and what can you do about it?

Every parent's dream is to be able to give your child the opportunity to succeed. Many parents have stated, "I just want my kids to be happy." And the last thing we want is for our children to be hurt or to suffer. Unfortunately, most of life's lessons are only learned the hard way, by failing or "skinning your knees." When we make it too easy for our children, these lessons are not learned— and in your family business environment, this will create nothing but problems. Any parents dealing with children who have a sense of entitlement or enablement wish they had approached things differently.

"I never want to rob my kids of the opportunity to fail," exclaimed one of our business owner clients. How very wise and profound on his part! He fully understands that most of our growth as individuals comes from our response to failure. It has been said, "The problem isn't getting knocked down; it's what you do to get back up." That's how your children will learn and become capable successors.

I've watched this wise business owner weather many storms over the years with his children. Although it's been painful, he has stuck to his resolve and let them work through issues, while loving and supporting them. Thankfully his children have overcome many challenges and are now active, productive managers in their dynamically growing business.

What's the American Dream? To give your children a better life than the one you grew up with. For many of our clients, they started at the bottom, or at least they could see the bottom. But their success has led to a very different lifestyle for their children, full of opportunities and experiences that they were thrilled to be able to provide.

One client remarked, "My son has never experienced anything other than first class." Clearly this business owner's comment reflected his understanding that his children will never have his perspective on how hard it is to make money and how vulnerable he feels at times financially, despite his tremendous success.

**Start by setting the ground rules with a Family Business Employment Policy.**

Since your business demands excellence in performance, how do you prevent entitlement from adversely affecting your children and your business?

Start by setting the ground rules. A Family Business Employment Policy is designed to help you put on paper what is required of any family member wishing to be employed by your company. Some of the criteria often included by business owners in this policy are: applying as any non-family applicant, completing a college degree, a satisfactory record of employment for two years working outside your business, a job opening available at your business suitable to the applicant's qualifications. None of these are cast in stone, and you will need to decide what will work in your family business. But remember, the easier you make it for your kids, the more likely they are to get infected with the "entitlement disease."

Why is work experience before they come into your business so important? Your child likely grew up around your business, so he/she is well known among your employees. It's often hard for your child to overcome the stigma of being the boss's kid. For many, immature actions while growing up, possibly when working after school or during the summers, have created impressions that stick.

Working somewhere else first allows your child to grow up and learn what it means to be an employee at a business that doesn't care who they are. In other words, they are going to have to earn the respect of those with whom they are working. And this can be a real confidence boost as he/she develops a skill set that will allow them to be productive immediately when they do come to work in your business.

What happens once your children start working in your business? The problem of trying to mentor your own son/daughter was summed up by one business owner when he told me, "I'm a softy—I know I let my son get away with murder." Being too hard on your kids can also create family problems, but usually it is the other way around—being too soft often creates entitlement and enablement, and you have to suffer the consequences.

**Set the expectations and write them down in a Family Business Expectations Policy.**

Set the expectations and write them down. A Family Business Expectations Policy is designed to clarify what you expect of your children when they work in your business. Attitude, work ethic, how they will be paid (based on the work they are doing), and the importance of them setting the right example are all keys to this document. You want your children to understand that first impressions matter, and if they are going to succeed, they have to earn respect from the other employees.

So, what do you do if you have already traveled down this path and are dealing with children who don't get it? One of our clients had the answer when he said, "If you see a turtle sitting on a fence post, you know it didn't get there by itself—someone had to put it there. I know my kid has entitlement issues, and I'm the one who let it happen, so I need to fix it." That admission was crucial to his commitment to addressing the issues with his child. It was painful as he started to challenge his child to earn his stripes instead of allowing him to go on feeling like he was entitled to be the successor. But, as a result, his child may have a future and possibly one day earn the right to be the leader of the company. Entitlement issues are tough, so you have to be tougher if you want your child to succeed.

## TOO TOUGH OR TOO EASY?

"I'm afraid I'll either be too tough or too easy on my son," lamented my mentor when discussing why he hadn't encouraged his son to join our succession planning business. Having worked with hundreds of family business owners, he understood how easy it is to be too focused on either *business first* or *family first* when dealing with family members in your business. But, regardless of how you approach training your child, the goal is to prepare your successor to be capable of running the business if you get hit by a bus today. Therefore, the question is "Is your successor ready?" If the answer is no, what needs to happen?

**The business owner always wears two hats: parent and business leader.**

Let's start by addressing one of your big challenges. As a father (or mother), the business owner always wears two hats: parent and business leader. All too often my partners and I at The Rawls Group are involved in coaching business owners who have wonderful intentions but fall prey to being either too easy or too hard on their child. If your child is going to be ready to be your successor, it's important to remember that you can give your child a job, a title, even a paycheck, but you can't give them respect—they have to earn it.

Recently when dealing with two brothers who each have sons in their business, it became apparent they each believed they had to advocate on behalf of their individual son, to protect their son's future in their company. I said, "I fully understand as a father why you want to protect your child and help him succeed, but your sons are men, not children—they don't need your protection." By protecting your child, you're hurting them and jeopardizing the business since you aren't forcing them to do the difficult things you had to do to succeed.

Each successor candidate needs to earn their position, demonstrating via their work ethic, teamwork, attitude, leadership, and performance that they have earned the respect of the management team, who will then want them to lead the company. Otherwise, once you are gone, it's only a matter of time before the talented managers are gone. They don't need to work for your son or daughter!

## What Are the Land Mines You Need to Avoid So Your Successor Succeeds?

It's such a temptation for parents to allow their children to skip steps that are vital to the development of your successor. The International Succession Planning Association® has identified seven C's that are essential to the development of successful leaders:

1. **Character:** Showing up on time, working hard, being responsible
2. **Capacity:** The ability to relate to people, adapting to other styles and personalities

**3. Commitment:** Elimination of alternatives—both feet in—no holding back

Demonstrating Character, Capacity, and Commitment are prerequisites to being an employee capable of being a candidate for management.

**4. Confidence:** "I know what I'm doing, and I can help you do it."
**5. Competence:** Skill sets in managing others, conflict management, accountability

Demonstrating Confidence and Competence are prerequisites to being a manager, capable of being a leader.

**6. Caring:** The human element—the people reporting to you are not just pawns to accomplish your goals but people with whom you are committed beyond work.
**7. Community:** Commitment and alignment to family, your work family, and communities—recognizing we're all in this together.

Demonstrating Caring and Community is what separates leaders from the rest of the pack!

So, how is your successor going to learn and demonstrate the seven C's of leadership?

## Take the Stairs Instead of the Elevator to the Top

Several years ago, I met with a business owner who for years had been extremely successful, with nary a blip in annual record profits. Then he hired his son! Things began to change as the father quickly promoted his son, frustrating the highly qualified, proven management. Before long, the son was given way too much authority and titles beyond his capabilities and experience. He began throwing his weight around. The manager most responsible for record profits decided he'd had enough and went to work for the competitor. It didn't take long before others began to follow, and soon the core managers were working for the competitor. Financial disaster followed quickly. Dad's unwillingness to deal with his son, promoting him without merit and without any indication of the son demonstrating the seven C's, was ruining his company.

It is crucial for your son/daughter to learn the basics of the business in order to earn respect. If your child is really capable, they will want to progress quickly and may feel like you are holding them back. That's a good problem. That is why it is extremely important that you develop a Successor Development Curriculum (explained later in this chapter) so your children can see where they are headed and what they have to do to move forward. This curriculum needs to include objectives/goals and measures of accountability so there are objective means of everyone knowing what progress is being made by your hopeful successor.

Promoting someone too quickly is a recipe for disaster as they are bypassing crucial learning benchmarks needed to sustain long-term productivity, especially in difficult market conditions they will eventually experience. Once promoted, no one wants to go backward to pick up this crucial knowledge and experience. Remember, some things can only be learned via experience— moving your successor too quickly bypasses experience and is often a detour to disaster. There is no shortcut to experience.

## Earn Their Pay and Title Like Everyone Else

"But I want my daughter to be able to afford a house in my neighborhood." This is understandable; you want your child to be able to share the good life you have earned, and you certainly want the best education for your grandchildren, usually meaning private school tuition. While your intentions are honorable, there are other ways of providing income rather than via their pay plan, which will be seen by other employees and affect how they view your child. Augmenting your child's income via your outside investments, real estate, etc. will prevent undermining their position in the company. When you pay too much or promote too quickly, this does not help your son/daughter become the leader you want them to be.

> **One hundred percent of those children of business owners who fail usually do so because one or more of the "successor rules" were violated.**

## Leadership Requires Respect, Which Is Earned

While many successful business owners and their successors have not followed the above "successor rules," it is no surprise that those who are talented, committed, hardworking, and self-motivated will usually succeed. Unfortunately, I have been brought in many times to resolve issues in family businesses where the above "rules" were violated and havoc reigned supreme. It is my experience that 100 percent of those children of business owners who fail usually do so because one or more of the above "successor rules" were violated.

There are a million rationalizations on why "my child" doesn't need a lot of experience:

*"She gets it."*

*"He's a natural."*

*"All my managers love her."*

*"I had to do it when I was young."*

Remember, your goal is to prepare your child to succeed when you are gone. Don't short-circuit the process—experience takes time.

# WILL YOUR SUCCESSOR BE READY?

I saw a cartoon recently in which the owner of a business said to his son as they gazed out of the window on the family business, "Someday, son, this will all be yours, unless I can come up with a better solution!"

That statement echoes the sentiment of many business owners I've worked with who are worried their son or daughter is not prepared to be able to lead the company if something happens to them.

How would you answer the following question? "Is your successor identified, trained, approved by the manufacturer/s (if applicable), respected by management, and able to run the company successfully today?" If your son or daughter is not ready today, you may determine to utilize a key manager via a Succession Bridge® until he/she is ready. Unfortunately, most business owners would answer the question about a qualified successor with a resounding "no" or a weak "I hope so"—neither of which is a satisfactory answer.

**The disciplines involved in getting a college education are more important than any individual class they may take.**

No one intentionally sets up their child for failure! But many business owners do so by not forcing their child to do the things necessary to prepare them for leadership. So, how do you prepare your child for success?

## Get Educated

This seems basic, but all too often children are able to convince their parents that education isn't important since "Dad doesn't have a college degree!" In today's world, an education is more important than ever. The disciplines involved in getting a college education are more important than any individual class they may take. This education needs to also involve industry training, available through outside organizations, such as the NADA Dealer Academy, the NCM Institute, Northwood University, and manufacturer programs.

## Work Somewhere Else First

Why? Because you will learn what it means to be an employee where your name doesn't give you any advantages and hopefully no one will cut you any slack. My partners and I at The Rawls Group strongly recommend your child work a minimum of one to two years for another company, which requires them to succeed on their own, developing confidence that's harder to get when they are working in your company. To many, this may sound like reasonable advice, but regularly we have to challenge business owners not to cut corners, which often happens when their child pushes back, saying, "You didn't work somewhere else" or "You didn't finish college" or "I can't be away from family to go for training classes."

One dealer that I have worked with for over thirty years was so excited about the prospect of his son joining him in the business after college. "We're going to be partners, working side by side together" was his viewpoint, so he resisted my advice to have his son work somewhere else first.

His son came into the family business right out of college and had trouble establishing himself with the senior management team, most of whom had known the son all his life and merely viewed him as the boss's kid. As a result, he floundered—and finally Dad was willing to listen.

We decided that since the Used Car department was the weak link in his dealership, he would send his son to a Twenty Group dealer friend in another state, who did a great job with used cars.

After a year the son returned, but now he brought knowledge that no one else had in their family dealership.

His understanding of how to run a great Used Car department helped build his confidence, and he began to act like a leader, which gained him respect. His world had changed, and his chances of becoming Dad's successor had improved exponentially. Fast-forward fifteen years, and this son is the proven award-winning Dealer Operator of his family business!

## Successor Development Curriculum

When a successor candidate comes on board, they need a plan that maps out the pathway to becoming a potential successor. This entails orienting them to all departments of your business so they can experience what employees must deal with.

This curriculum should include the learning objectives in which they need to demonstrate proficiency in each department before being moved to the next one. Estimated time frames will help give them an understanding of what it will take to achieve their objective of becoming your successor. Ultimately, the goal is for them to demonstrate they have the knowledge required and the leadership ability to be able to step into your shoes when the time comes.

All too often business owners cut corners, allowing their children to take the elevator to the top when they need to take the stairs. Bottom line: this curriculum is designed to help your successor discover their natural aptitudes applicable to the business and be prepared to lead others who complement their skill sets.

"What are we preparing your successor for?" asked my Rawls Group business partner Jeff Faulkner as we began discussions regarding the expected onboarding of the next generation. For many of our clients, their goal is to be General Manager of one store. But their success has often multiplied the size of their business exponentially. As a result, Generations 2 and 3 in this situation would need to be prepared to lead a billion-dollar business. This would clearly take a very different approach to the successor's development.

Unfortunately, business is a combat sport! To succeed, your successor needs to be prepared to deal with well-financed, effective competitors who will not treat your child with kid gloves. Your successor will need to learn how to deal with adversity; they will need to learn how to lead so others will follow—even when times are tough, and the odds of success may seem overwhelming.

When your child pushes back and doesn't want to do the hard things required to succeed, as the business owner and parent, you must stand tall. Your decisions will impact whether your successor is ready today.

## SUCCEEDING THE OLD-FASHIONED WAY: SHE EARNED IT

The look on my face when the fifty-four-year-old dealer told me that he was promoting his twenty-eight-year-old daughter to be the GM was a dead giveaway. "Why is that a problem? I was a GM at that age," he said. And obviously it worked out great for this dealer, so why was I questioning his decision to promote his daughter? The issue, I told him, is that he grew up in an entirely different set of circumstances than the world his daughter experiences, and the maturity levels created by such are hard to replicate.

I explained, "When you started out, you didn't have two extra nickels." "Yes," he said, "I sold my house and invested every dollar I had in getting my first store." "That's my point, I said, "You had to succeed; you didn't have a choice. There was no safety net if you failed."

As a result, this business owner was handling his finances with mirrors, hoping the receivables could keep up with the payables. He worked in every part of the dealership, with his hands on everything. He didn't question staying late, working extra hours, doing whatever it took to find a way to sell one more car so that he could make payroll. He trained all his people to watch expenses and to complete the paperwork correctly the first time so that banks responded quickly. Everyone knew that there was no sugar daddy to rely on if times got tough and sales began to slide.

Over time, due to hard work, some luck, the development of solid business practices, and more hard work, this dealer's store began to make money. Being conservative, he plowed most of his profits back into his company, knowing that this was the only way to grow and build financial strength in order to survive adversity. Over time, his capital accounts began to grow, and one day, his accountant even remarked that he was over-capitalized.

One day, along comes his daughter, eager to follow in his footsteps. He is immensely proud and excited that his dream of working together appears to be fulfilled. He wants her to learn the business, but there is a part of him that is conflicted. On the one hand, he knows that most learning is caught not taught, and she will have to pay her dues. But, he doesn't necessarily want her to have to struggle as much as he did. She wants more family time, and that makes sense

**You don't necessarily want her to have to struggle as much as you did.**

to him since he has some guilt about the long hours he put in when she was growing up. He rationalizes that she is bright, hardworking, and can learn the business faster than he did.

As a result, he short-circuited the training process, moving her through the departments over months, not years. He even sent her to the NADA Academy, because he heard how effective this training is for potential dealers. So, the next thing you know, she moves through the ranks as a manager—three months in Used Cars, six months in Finance & Insurance. Then the General Sales Manager quits, so Dad decides to let his daughter have a shot at it—she's energetic and full of confidence. Before too long, he's convinced himself that she can run her own store—at age twenty-eight!

So, what's wrong with this picture? Maybe nothing, as anyone in the car business can point to many success stories that started out this way. But what was different between Dad's situation and his daughter's? As stated above, Dad *had* to be successful because there was no safety net.

But his daughter knows that Dad is right behind her and isn't going to let her fail. The store that she is running is well capitalized, so there is a lot of money and some strong managers to prop her up when needed. Based on this, she may seem to succeed while times are good and the money is plentiful. But the car business is tough, and sooner or later she is going to face tough times. When that happens, will she be ready? Will she have the emotional toughness to be able to make the hard decisions, to watch the expenses closely, to be creative and work extra hours and do whatever it takes to succeed in a tough economy or with a less than stellar brand?

> **His daughter knows that Dad is right behind her and isn't going to let her fail.**

All too often, I see the children of dealers think they know what they are doing, but obviously they lack the maturity created by learning the old-fashioned way—by earning their position. When looking at the training necessary to be effective as a dealer for the long haul, don't short-circuit your children by promoting them too quickly.

Contrast this approach to several daughters with whom I've worked, who are well on their way to becoming successors ready and able to lead their companies. There was plenty of temptation to move them quickly through the ranks, as their education and workplace experience were exemplary. But fortunately for them, their parents understand the long game they are playing.

The management teams the daughters would be responsible for needed to know they had served alongside them in the trenches and earned their stripes. "She understands the challenges we face daily" is the compliment they now receive, whether spoken or unspoken. Experience has earned each of these women the credentials necessary to be leaders and successor owners in their companies. No doubt they didn't like having to work long hours and take extra shifts because the department was shorthanded, but they did it and are now reaping the rewards of this extra effort.

**If your legacy is going to continue successfully through the next generation, your children are going to have to *earn* it.**

Some very important lessons have been learned in the trenches, as they are getting their hands dirty and paying their dues. The employees respect their hard work and know their boss knows what she is talking about because she's been where they are.

It's easy to give in and bend the rules when dealing with issues regarding your children working in your business. But in the end, if your legacy is going to continue successfully through the next generation, your children are going to have to *earn* it.

# 3

# Communication Challenges

"What part of **NO** don't you understand?!?"

# Time Bomb #3

# Family Communication Challenges

## "WHY DOESN'T HE UNDERSTAND ME?"

"I'm a direct and clear communicator, so why doesn't my son understand what I'm saying?" exclaimed the frustrated business owner father to me. "We seem to have the same conversations but get nowhere."

This same father would be the first to admit that he and his son are very different, but he has not yet come to the conclusion that the filters through which each of them are communicating are vastly different. This is completely normal—within each family there are often similarities but also significant differences in how we communicate.

We tend to assume that "since I've known my family member all my life, I know what he/she thinks and how to communicate with this person." But history teaches us our assumptions regarding family communication are often incorrect, leading to disharmony and dysfunction. When you bring this into the heat of a family business, eruptions often occur.

To help our family business clients communicate more effectively, my partners and I at The Rawls Group utilize a personality-profile, strengths-based analysis called ProScan®. This has some similarity to other models such as DiSC®, Wilson Learning®, and Myers-Briggs MBTI®. ProScan® is an extremely helpful tool for families and others working together to better understand what makes the other person tick and what each needs to be aware of when dealing with their family members (and non-family member employees).

We've all heard the expression "It's nothing personal, just business." For some people, that's perfectly true, while for others, like me, "Everything feels personal"—that's both my strength and weakness. I'm focused on people and get my energy from people. That's good, but the challenge is that I can get my feelings hurt too easily, I have a need to feel connected, and I may have problems with confrontation because I want people to like me.

One business owner with a similar personality likes to complain, "My daughter [who is the COO] doesn't talk to me, and she doesn't spend enough time with the employees. Why doesn't she just call me once in a while to let me know what she's doing?" This daughter is highly effective and respected by the management team she leads, but her style of communicating is different from her father's.

She is more of a numbers person, organized, strategic, delegating, and task focused, while Dad is more hands-on, engages with their employees, gets involved in all the details. Is one of them leading the wrong way? No! Father and daughter are both extremely effective and productive—but different—leaders, and their differences tend to cause friction between them.

To improve their relationship, she needs to make more time for her father, and he needs to accept that it isn't personal when she doesn't call. She assumes if she is doing a good job, she is meeting his expectations. Dad needs to accept that her style may be very different from his, but it's working as seen in the numbers she and her team produce.

In another family business, the son was so frustrated. "My dad is a control freak! He only wants to do it his way. I can't get him to listen to my opinion." There's a street in every city named after this guy: One Way. I explained to him that to get his father to listen, he needs to give him options, not tell him what to do.

My younger brother is a very successful doctor and by personality a dominant person who also likes to be in control. The last thing he wants is for his older brother to tell him what to do. But when I'm smart enough to couch my proposal in terms of options, he is much more willing to listen because he gets the final say. I determined the options, so it's a win-win environment. If only I could remember to do this all the time.

One business owner and his son's differences are based on how much importance each of them places on structure, processes, and procedures. When given a task, the father wants to know, "Have we done this before? If yes, do we have a process and procedure we can continue to follow? If it ain't broke, why fix it?" The father learned the business in a very structured environment: "If you simply follow our rules for success, you will succeed," which he did.

The son just wants to know what you want him to accomplish. "Don't tell me how to do it. I'm creative, and I'll figure it out—and oh, by the way, I'll probably figure out a better way of doing it."

This difference in their personalities was a constant source of friction and frustration between them. Dad insisted his son do it Dad's way, which was to follow his rules (which, to Dad, meant the difference between success and failure). Everyone I spoke with who knew the situation believed the son was a more effective leader than his father, but Dad's unwillingness to allow for a different approach was destructive to his son and to their business.

What happens when a structured person is working with a more spontaneous person? Sometimes, it is the little things on which we differ that drive family members crazy, especially those working together.

I am a very spontaneous person. To combat this tendency, I need to work very hard at creating structure and staying organized. But if I get a call from a client, I'm quick to take the call and focus on that person's situation. That's a strength but also has the potential to be my weakness. The client is happy because I responded quickly. But my partner may not be as happy. Why?

I'm likely to immediately respond to the client's question by barging into my partner's office and saying, "Jeff, I just got a call from our client, and we need to respond." Jeff is a more organized, structured person, whose first thought (we've talked about this many times) is "Why are you assuming this is more important than the things I'm working on?" Instead of a positive reaction, I'm more likely to frustrate him. A much better approach would be to text him or just ask, "When can I get a few minutes to discuss the call I just got from our client?" Jeff now has time to prioritize what he is doing while still addressing our client's issue.

Many times I've heard someone say in an exasperated tone of voice, "You just said it; you must have meant it!" This statement exposes a difference between those who think internally and those who think externally.

I'm an external thinker while my partner Jeff Bannon is an internal thinker. So, when we first started working together twelve years ago, I would come into his office and start talking about how we should approach a client situation. He would listen and maybe nod, and after a few minutes I would assume he was agreeing and say, "So, you agree that's what we should do." "No, I don't agree," he'd reply. "I was just nodding to let you know I heard what you said. I may come to the same conclusion, but I have to think it over."

For those of us who are external thinkers, we do our best thinking when in dialogue with someone. That seems crazy to internal thinkers, who want time to process their thoughts. Internal thinkers are usually careful communicators who measure what they say before saying it. Jeff likes to say internal thinkers tend to picture themselves when they speak as opening a door and locking it behind them—whatever they say is now out there permanently; they can't take it back.

Jeff describes external thinkers as communicating through a swinging door, where they are not as concerned about reversing what they said. To those of us external thinkers, we have all experienced a situation in which, as words came out of our mouth, they clarified our thinking, and we said, "That's a bad idea!" On the spot, we reversed ourselves (through the swinging door). "You said it; you must have meant it" makes sense to an internal thinker but is less true for those of us external thinkers.

You are likely to be working with family and non-family who think differently than you, either externally or internally. What do you need to remember in order to be more effective working together?

External thinkers need responses to do their best thinking. They love to play conversational ping-pong: "I like your idea, and what if we did this . . . ?" "That would work, and what if we added this . . . ?" So, when I'm speaking with Jeff, I want him to give me some idea of what he is thinking. Since he is concerned with not saying something he hasn't thought through properly, he will often reply, "This isn't my final thought, but here is my first reaction," which gives him some allowance to be able to respond, knowing it is important to me to get some feedback.

Internal thinkers need time to think things through before responding. So, I need to shut up and wait for Jeff to respond. He has tremendous wisdom and, given time to think things through, will likely come to a very prudent and creative decision.

Jeff is much more inclined to be a "ready, ready, aim, aim, fire" type of decision-maker, which means he might err in the amount of time needed to make a decision, but he makes very few bad decisions. I tend to be more of a "ready, fire, aim" decision-maker, meaning I can make decisions very quickly but can get myself in trouble by responding before evaluating properly. I must be extra careful with important decisions, especially when the consequences are not easily reversible. (I've simplified both Jeff's and my approaches to decision-making here to help make my point.)

Several years ago, I was meeting with a business owner client for the first time. He admitted that he was a quick decision-maker, and to compensate, he held himself to a rule that he'd sleep on any big decision. He told me, "I'm probably going to hire you, but I'm going to let you know tomorrow." I'm grateful for this advice that I try to practice and for the years we were able to work together.

It is very easy to assume that since you and your family grew up in the same household, you obviously know how to communicate effectively with each other. This is not always true! And that's why assumptions can and will create misunderstandings among you and your family members.

When I first came into the succession planning business, my partners and I utilized the Wilson Learning® system to help us understand how to communicate more effectively with our clients. This breaks down personality traits into four quadrants. Just to show you that God has a sense of humor, in my primary family, my mother, father, brother, and I were each in one of the four quadrants—we are very different. Communication was challenging. That may be the case in your family, too.

Family business requires family to communicate often under the intense pressures of business. The more you understand each other—learning how you are different and respecting each other's differences—and the more you are willing to pay attention to what's important to each personality when communicating, the less tension and the fewer inaccurate assumptions you will experience, resulting in a more harmonious and productive family and business.

## ATTITUDE IS EVERYTHING

According to Andre Agassi in his Canon commercial in 1990, "Image is everything!" But in business, especially when times get tough, attitude will be far more important to the survival of your business. The same is true for your child who is hoping to be your successor. Attitude communicates loud and clear—positively or negatively—and a bad attitude is hard to overcome.

There are a lot of things the owners of family businesses don't control: the economy, interest rates, tariffs, lenders, inventory supply lines. But you do control your attitude, and that can have a huge impact on how you respond to business crisis, which is inevitable.

A few years ago, I was speaking with a car dealer in Buffalo, and I casually commented that it must be tough trying to sell cars in Buffalo in January and February. His eyes lit up, and he slammed his fist on the desk and said dramatically, "That's when I grab market share!" Clearly, he was not going to let himself or his people succumb to the "woe is me" syndrome. He obviously does not control the weather, but his attitude is one of finding ways to win despite the adverse circumstances. As a result, he not only grabs market share, but his store consistently is a sales leader in the country during these months.

Staying positive is often difficult to do, especially when we are barraged by negative news. Not only are you as the business owner impacted by this, but all your employees as well. At times it seems everyone wants to share with you how bad things are: "You think your situation is bad—you should see what I have to deal with." As a result, it is easy to get sucked into gloom and doom thinking, which tends to debilitate your productivity. At that point it feels like you are walking in quicksand, and your energy is drained. Fortunately, this is not a feeling that you don't control but rather *an attitude that you do control.*

Having a positive attitude is not going to fix an economic crisis (nor the turmoil we experienced with COVID). But without a positive attitude, it is almost impossible to address any problem, especially a crisis of this magnitude. A positive attitude has the ability—better than anything else—to lift you, your family, and your business, and it is critical when you are going through trials. If you demonstrate a positive attitude toward your family and employees, you have given them a gift that is priceless.

> **If you demonstrate a positive attitude toward your family and employees, you have given them a gift that is priceless.**

Your children need to know they have total control of their attitude. This may sound crazy to you, and when I was told that by a therapist, I thought he didn't know what he was talking about. There are times when I have felt down, depressed, and experienced a general feeling of "no one understands what I'm going through or feeling." So, how was I in control?

Negative emotions can feel overwhelming. At times, with all the uncertainties of business, health issues, finances, and the world seeming upside down, it's easy to feel like "I've had it, and I deserve to feel down and depressed." Emotions can be contagious. As leaders, we know if we don't stay upbeat and encouraged, how can we expect our team members to cope and be positive at work?

You must believe you have total control of your attitude. Don't believe me? For years I didn't believe that. I was world-class at acting like a martyr, especially around my family, where I probably thought I could get away with it—"Woe is me . . . poor me . . . nobody understands my situation." I would often feel overwhelmed and couldn't be positive. A friend helped me understand that wasn't true. When you are having a bad day and get a call from someone important to you, you immediately respond, "Hi, Tom, I'm doing great. How about you?" I realized I *do* have control over my attitude. So, as the leader of your family business, you can decide to stay upbeat and positive—and you must—especially in difficult times. Your children need to know this, and they need to see you modeling a positive attitude.

There are a lot of things that affect our emotions. To stay upbeat and positive, get extra rest, eat right, exercise, and pray—staying mentally and emotionally sharp demands this. Staying positive so those around you can feed off your enthusiasm is one key thing; understanding and empathy are also critical. Each person deals with stress differently, and those around you have problems and challenges that may be overwhelming to them: financial, health, family, fear of losing their job. Now more than ever, people need to know you care. In the middle of your day, are you willing to take time to check in with your people? Are you approachable? There is nothing like asking a person, "George, are you doing okay?" in a tone that says, "I really want to know."

What is the one thing you need to communicate to your children if you want them to succeed in your family business? Bring the right attitude to

**Bring the right attitude to work every day—can do, will do, and you can count on me.**

work every day—can do, will do, and you can count on me. This positive attitude will take you a long way down the road to success. What does attitude have to do with business succession? Everything!

The following quote from author and pastor Chuck Swindoll sums up beautifully how important attitude is in all of life:

> The longer I live, the more I realize the impact of attitude on life. Attitude, to me, is more important than facts. It is more important than the past, than education, than money, than circumstances, than failures, than successes, than what other people think or say or do. It is more important than appearance, giftedness or skill. It will make or break a company . . . a church . . . a home. The remarkable thing is we have a choice every day regarding the attitude we will embrace for that day. We cannot change our past. We cannot change the fact that people will act in a certain way. We cannot change the inevitable. The only thing we can do is play on the one string we have, and that is our attitude. I am convinced that life is 10 percent what happens to me and 90 percent how I react to it. And so it is with you. We are in charge of our attitudes.

## FEAR: THE BIG MOTIVATOR

What does fear have to do with successful business owners? *A lot!*

How can that be? We're talking about the titans of industry, the leaders of the community, the heroes to many, the self-made success stories, the financial giants. How could they possibly fear anything?

It takes a unique personality to be an entrepreneur, willing to go out on a limb and risk everything financially to achieve your dream. It's not for the faint of heart! This person—man or woman—has guts and the willingness to stick their head in the lion's mouth. This is the person who achieves dreams, impacts communities, and builds empires. They come in all sizes and shapes, ages and genders, but each one has a dream and the commitment to make it happen. So how could this person ever be fearful?

Family members have probably never considered that, as the owner of the family business, Dad or Mom could possibly grapple with fear. Just maybe, if they understood this, they could appreciate what motivates their parents and try to extend grace when the impacting behaviors frustrate family members.

*"My dad works too hard."*

*"I never get enough of Mom's time."*

*"Dad won't give up control."*

*"Mom is so driven to succeed, which drives me crazy."*

Sound familiar? Family frustrations are real.

*"Quit your complaining. I've provided you a great lifestyle,"* said the business owner.

How do these tension-filled moments happen in successful family business environments? Because successful people pay a price to achieve success, and family members experience the consequences of your sacrifices. (They also reap the benefits!)

All too often, misconceptions influence the relationship between the owner and his/her children. "All he cares about is keeping control" is a phrase I've heard countless times. The assumption is that the owner is unwilling to let go, unwilling to give up the position of power. "Dad's total focus is on business and nothing else." Often the child assumes Dad does so only for his own satisfaction.

**Could it be, despite a multimillion-dollar portfolio and a business generating millions, the owner continues to fear losing it all?**

What does this have to do with *fear*? Everything! Rarely does anyone ask *why*?

*"Why does Dad work so hard?"*

*"Why does Mom want to stay in control?"*

Could it be, despite a multimillion-dollar portfolio and a business generating millions, the owner continues to fear losing it all? This seems crazy, but I know from working with so many business owners that the fear of failure is real.

Fear of failure doesn't necessarily mean fear of bankruptcy. But when you've attained a level of prestige in your community and enjoy a lifestyle to which you've become accustomed, there can be a real fear of going backward.

*"What will people think if we have to downsize?"*

*"What if we have to sell one of our companies?"*

*"Will our bankers still believe in us?"*

*"Will I have to lay off many employees who depend on me?"*

> **So why does the owner work so hard? Why is he unavailable for family events?**

One owner told me years ago, "I've been rich, and I've been poor—rich is better!" You remember your past, but financially you don't want to return to it.

COVID brought fear to many family business owners. Fear was also a dominant motivator during the economic collapse of 2008 and 2009. The impact of tariffs caused family business owners to see profits tumble, again causing fear in many strong family business owners. The electrification of the auto industry has resulted in many dealers selling out, fearful of the future of their business. Every family business owner is very aware of the vagaries of business and how easily fortunes can be lost. Owners will rarely admit out loud that they fear failure, but I've had enough heart-to-heart conversations to know this is a fact.

So why does the owner work so hard? Why is he unavailable for family events? Why is she so focused and possibly intense? Why does she struggle to give up control and not let the next generation take over?

*"If I lose my intensity or take time off or give up control, my dream company may implode or just begin to lose its effectiveness."*

*"What if my kids don't work hard enough, and the business fails?"*

*"I'd better keep my foot on the pedal and my hands on the wheel so our business can stay in the fast lane and not end up in the ditch."*

Fear of failure is a huge motivator. It gets you up in the morning when others are sleeping in; it causes you to burn the midnight oil; it creates a lot of sleepless nights; it creates stress and results in behaviors that can be damaging to family relationships.

*"But so many people are depending on me."*

*"My competitors are breathing down my neck."*

*"If my company doesn't continue to grow, it will be on the way to dying."*

These are heavy burdens that family business owners carry daily.

"Okay, Hugh, I get it. Dad's under a lot of pressure, but I have to live with the consequences. I'd just like to get more time with my dad." This is what your child is feeling and something as parents we must not lose sight of.

**Business owners can then lose sight of the fears of their family.**

Most children of family business owners want a close relationship with their parent yet may feel that "Dad or Mom doesn't have time for me; the demands of the family business are just too great." As the parent, you may not be aware of the unavailability vibe you are projecting to your children. And it's likely the opposite of how you want to be with your children. But in our high-paced lifestyle and with the demands of business, many of the children of business owners with whom I've worked feel it's tough to get the amount of time they want with their parent.

Fear of failure can cause us to be laser focused, which is often a huge factor in the success of family businesses. Business owners can then lose sight of the fears of their family—"The business is robbing me of my relationship with my dad or mom."

I wish there were easy answers. Overcoming fear and its effect on your family usually requires you to admit it first to yourself and, if possible, to your family. What an incredibly brave thing that would be for you to admit to your family that you struggle to be both a successful business owner and a loving parent, involved in the lives of your children and grandchildren.

Just maybe, this would open up the lines of communication, raising not lowering your stature in their eyes, allowing your family members to get closer to you. We all have fears, and they impact our behavior. Acknowledging this to those you love creates vulnerability. Hopefully it will also create the ability to talk with your family about what is important, creating stronger family relationships. Isn't that what we want?

The statement "You can't take it with you" is true. Success in relationships lasts forever. Do you fear failure in relationships as much as you fear failure in your business?

# 4

# **Children Are Not Equal**

"Was this Dad's idea of equal partners?"

# Time Bomb #4

# *Children Are* Not *Equal*

## "I LOVE MY KIDS EQUALLY, BUT THEY DON'T PRODUCE EQUALLY"

"How do I resolve this issue? If I don't address this, there will be a mess after I'm gone, but if I open up this can of worms, my life may be hell and my family will be in an uproar." I asked this frustrated business owner if he was paying his sons the same amount, and unsurprisingly, he said, "Yes." "Do they own equal amounts of stock?" I asked. Again, the answer was yes. Clearly, he had identified the problem but did not know how to resolve it. In over forty years of working with family business owners, I have heard this story retold many times. Why? What is the impact upon succession planning?

> "If I don't address this, there will be a mess after I'm gone, but if I open up this can of worms, my life may be hell and my family will be in an uproar."

When dealing with family members, owners often disregard sound business practice, making decisions from the heart instead of doing what is best for the business. Ironically, this usually backfires, creating family problems on top of business problems. Equal pay plans regardless of responsibility or productivity, promoting children before they are ready or qualified, allowing children to operate in a freelance style, coming and going as they please, are behaviors my partners and I see all the time in family businesses.

When your child began working in your business, were you willing to apply the same ground rules that you would if he/she was not related? For instance, did your son/daughter have to qualify for a job in your business using the same basis as a non-relative who applies? Would his/her résumé qualify your child to be given their initial job? Future jobs?

> Sooner or later, the more productive child is not going to put up with equal pay and equal stock ownership when he/she is carrying the major load.

It is amazingly common for children to be paid the same, regardless of their position within the business. You certainly would not do this with employees who are not related to you. Undoubtedly, this happens because Dad is unwilling to make business decisions that appear like he is playing favorites. He may also feel pressure to help his children equally so that they can take care of their own families and have similar lifestyles. This is a problem that must be addressed *now* if you plan for your legacy to continue via your children. Sooner or later, the more productive child is not going to put up with equal pay and equal stock ownership when he/she is carrying the major load.

"Dad, I'm not going to be a fifty-fifty partner with my brother. That will never work!" Fortunately, this father listened to his son and allowed us to discuss and make changes to his estate plan as well as asset transfers that we were planning to complete. It wasn't easy, and we had to work to find solutions that would be acceptable to the family—but there was too much discrepancy between the contributions being made to the business by the two siblings, so fifty-fifty was not going to work. Thankfully, solutions were found before this family issue negatively impacted the business.

In most cases, the turmoil is brewing below the surface, but it will definitely boil over when Dad is gone—if not before. For the business succession plan to be successful, this issue needs to be resolved *now* while Dad is around to help reach a solution. Many business owners are reluctant to get into this discussion because they are fearful of not being able to find a solution without tearing apart the family. Unfortunately, unless Dad addresses the problem, his family—and often the business—will be torn apart after he is gone. Therefore, a third-party adviser is usually necessary to open up these potentially volatile issues and achieve amicable solutions.

**Unfortunately, unless Dad addresses the problem, his family—and often the business—will be torn apart after he is gone.**

A key to getting this problem resolved is to engage all the players in discussion regarding their expectations. What do you expect from your sibling? What should your sibling be able to expect from you? What should Mom or Dad be able to expect from each of their children who are working in the business? What should your children be able to expect from you? Values, job descriptions, roles and responsibilities, decision-making, communication, hours, authority, vacations, pay plans, stock ownership, bonuses—this all needs to be discussed, the more in detail the better, and the expectations need to be written down.

Often one or more parties perceive things entirely differently, and this will present problems. As a result, each of the parties is likely to have unreasonable expectations. This is where a third-party intermediary is critical, helping each of the siblings and the parent owner work through their differences. If done properly, this process will take several meetings, culminating in all parties signing what has been agreed upon. There is no shortcut if you want to find solutions that will work for everyone.

The stakes are very high—the future of your business and the ability of your family to enjoy harmonious relationships. Find someone soon who can help you tackle and resolve this crucial issue or risk having to sell your business in the future. What could possibly be more important?

## "I KNOW MY KIDS ARE DIFFERENT, BUT . . ."

You knew your children were different from the day they were born or soon after, yet in family businesses, I see parents trying to squeeze their sons and daughters into the same mold. "I don't know how to engage each of my children in my business. They all want to be employed here, but they don't all bring the same energy and drive, not to mention abilities. How do I make this work without messing up my business or family?"

This business owner is describing the family business challenges often encountered when you have multiple children who want to work in your company. Some children are more motivated and committed than their siblings. Some are hard workers but lack education and training. Some have lots of talent but their attitude is one of entitlement, so they're not willing to work hard or earn the right to be heard (but they think they know it all).

The challenge for lots of parents who own family businesses is how to support and encourage each of your children to be the best they can be, while not handicapping the business or overburdening your successor child. If one child has shown the drive, commitment, aptitude, attitude, work ethic, and talent to be a successor candidate and your other child has not, then you can't expect to put them on the same pathway to the top of your company.

All children should enter your business as an employee who must prove they have what it takes before being considered as a successor candidate. This means demonstrating the basic things required of every employee—coming to work on time, dressing appropriately, working hard, keeping a good attitude, demonstrating responsibility and reliability. In other words, earning the right to be considered for promotion. For some children, they do not have what it takes to become a successor candidate. You can't treat being a successor candidate as a birthright if you want what's best for your company.

**All children should enter your business as an employee who must prove they have what it takes before being considered as a successor candidate.**

Assuming your child has what it takes and has earned the right to become a successor candidate, they are on their way to becoming a leader within your company. The road to becoming a successor must be based on merit, not just because they have the same name as you. Now you must separate family from business decisions, allowing your children to rise only to the level they've earned.

"My daughter is the natural leader, and her brothers are not as committed to our business [meaning, they don't work very hard but have great golf handicaps]," explained the owner of a real estate development company. Fortunately, he recognized her capabilities and had designated her to be his successor. Unfortunately, he was allowing her brothers to ride her coattails, not carrying their share of the load. He was saddling his daughter with two anchors that she would have to drag behind her when he died.

What happens when you have a leader and a follower, and both are your children and both are involved in your business? You can't treat them the same, yet all too often that is exactly what happens. If one is carrying a bigger load, that person needs to be recognized and compensated accordingly.

> Entitlement usually rears its ugly head when decisions are not being based on merit but rather on being a member of the "lucky sperm club."

Often my partners and I enter the situation decades after the parents have equally transferred stock to their children via trusts for estate planning purposes. The expectation created is that each of their children is equally going to share in stock ownership. Entitlement usually rears its ugly head when decisions are not being based on merit but rather on being a member of the "lucky sperm club."

In many situations the disparity between the contributions of the siblings is huge. Not only is this unfair to the child who will be leading the company, but the parents have created a huge relationship burden for the successor child to carry. "Dad always favored you and gave you the opportunities." This perception is hard to overcome and may not be based on facts. There is no comeback for the successor child who must deal with the animosity created by his/her sibling. Usually, the follower child made life choices, such as a lack of education or training, that precluded them from getting ahead. The assumptions by parents that lead to these challenges is often rooted in the fear that "I want to be fair to all my children" and "I love all my children equally and don't want them to feel like I don't."

Business decisions regarding family don't have to be at the expense of doing what is best for your company. I have great respect and admiration for the business owner who shared the following with me.

"Two of my sons are clearly driven to succeed, capable, well educated, strategic thinkers, proven leaders, so it was natural to see them as my eventual successors. They work well together, and we are working to utilize each of their complementary skill sets for the betterment of the company. My other son has never expressed any interest in being involved at the leadership level but commands respect for his work ethic and commitment to the elbow-grease side of our business. All three will participate in stock ownership, but I've allocated stock ownership according to levels of responsibility, not because each is my son."

This father understands and appreciates the differences among his sons and wants them to feel loved and respected, regardless of what level of involvement they have in his company.

Your children are created in the image of God, but their differences must be respected and taken into account when making decisions regarding your business. If not, your family and your business will both suffer.

# 5

# Who Gets to Wear the Crown?

"I'm the boss - **NO** I am."

# Time Bomb #5

# *Sibling Partnerships = Fireworks?*

## WHO GETS TO WEAR THE CROWN?

During my first meeting with the business owner, he pointed to a picture of his son and daughter on his desk. The kids in the picture were five and six years old, and both were wearing golden paper crowns. He said, "It was the younger one's birthday, but the frown on my son's face made it clear he wanted to be the only one wearing the crown. That's still my problem today; they both work in my business, and both still want to be the one who wears the crown!"

He went on to say, "Neither one is willing to work for the other, and this has caused lots of sibling rivalry." His wife then said, "If this doesn't stop, we'll sell the business before we let it destroy our family."

The owner voiced his agreement with that sentiment and explained how

> "Neither one is willing to work for the other, and this has caused lots of sibling rivalry."

they had experienced tremendous family trauma with his father, so they were not going to let this happen again.

My partners and I have heard similar stories from business owners over and over again, but when it comes to the decision to actually sell, this is often hard to do, especially when most business owners love their business and don't want to sell. So, usually they do nothing, hoping this problem will solve itself somehow, someway.

> "I've got a real problem—I've got three sons, and in a business there can only be one boss. I'm going to have to make a decision, and when I do, two will be angry."

An owner of a manufacturing company told me, "I've got a real problem—I've got three sons, and in a business there can only be one boss. I'm going to have to make a decision, and when I do, two will be angry." He was voicing his version of the proverbial family business problem of choosing your successor.

He obviously cares about all his children, yet he doesn't want to make a decision that will jeopardize the future success of his business. And for many business owners in this situation, it gets further complicated by the fact that his wife may feel differently than he does as she may focus on what the impact will be on the family while he focuses more on the business impact. Not knowing what to do and not wanting to open a can of worms that may harm family relationships and negatively impact the business, the business owner usually does nothing, hoping the problem will solve itself somehow.

In a third situation I encountered, the auto dealer has one highly qualified child and one who is passionate about wanting to become the successor but may not have what it takes. The dealer said, "There is no way these two could work together, so I'll probably give two of my stores to each of them."

Obviously, this solves the problem of them working together, but it may also be setting the one child up for future failure if he is not able to run the dealerships. Again, Dad loves his children and wants to help both but is conflicted on how he can resolve this issue so that his family is not damaged and neither is his business.

So, how do you pick your successor without destroying your family? In each of the situations described above, the business owner was focusing on the end result, trying to make the decision *before* their child was ready.

The most important question is "Is your son or daughter capable of running the company today if something happened to you?" No one should be designated as your successor until they are ready and capable to run your operations effectively or, in the case of auto and truck dealers, to be approved by the manufacturer. In each of these situations, since none of the next generation were ready, I said, "Put that decision on the back burner and focus everyone's attention on getting your children prepared so all of your children will be successful."

One client's son asked, "Have you ever seen siblings able to run a family business successfully together?" My response was a resounding "Yes!" But, in order for this to work, both siblings have to be committed, willing to work hard, willing to work at communicating effectively with each other, respecting and affirming each other's contributions and differences, and not keeping score. The fact is, most siblings have skill sets that are complementary. To be successful, they will need someone like their sibling. If they can resolve the family issues, this type of partnership can be enormously successful.

However, this won't work for everyone. It would be the wrong move to put some siblings together. When this is the case, business owners often begin to look for opportunities to buy a second business or franchise to provide for each of their children. But unless you have determined that each of your children is committed and capable, focusing on buying a second business is putting the cart before the horse. It doesn't solve anything to put your child in a situation in which they will ultimately fail.

> Unless you have determined that each of your children is committed and capable, focusing on buying a second business is putting the cart before the horse.

When dealing with family, it is easy to let your natural desire to provide for your children overwhelm your business understanding of what is needed to be a successful business owner. You don't need to have been in business for very long to remember when your market tanked and you worried about becoming a casualty. Business is tough, and your children must have the capability to survive in a down market. The most important issue to resolve is whether your son or daughter is ready, willing, and able and if he/she has *earned* the right to wear the crown.

## MULTIPLE FAMILY SHAREHOLDERS

"I need operational control if our succession plan is going to work." This business owner was echoing the sentiment of so many others facing family business succession planning situations in which they know they will have to contend with minority shareholders who aren't involved in operations yet demand a say in what goes on—because "I own stock."

This is a tough one because it usually results from Mom and Dad wanting to treat their children equally and wanting to save on estate taxes. So, they've transferred stock, hopefully non-voting stock, to their active and inactive children. Now everyone is in the boat together, with multiple expectations as to what they should receive from the business.

All too often, this positions the family member who is running the business to be either the "bad king" or the "hand-cuffed operator"—neither extreme is desirable for the family or the business. So, the best way to position yourself and your successor is somewhere in the middle.

No one wants to run a business without the autonomy to make critical operational decisions. And no one wants to invest their assets in something they can't control or get out of when things go bad. Those active in running the business want authority to make decisions that are in the best interests of the company. Those shareholder family members not involved in operations want income and usually a say in the business decisions affecting them.

The simple solution is to set up a buy-sell agreement and give the active shareholders the right to buy out the inactive shareholders. That allows the business to be owned by those running it and decisions to reflect the best interests of the business.

**But often family priorities determine that inactive shareholders, who may have owned an interest in the business for years, have the option of remaining shareholders.**

But often family priorities determine that inactive shareholders, who may have owned an interest in the business for years, have the option of remaining shareholders. Now what do you do to make it work for all family members?

Priority number one is to make sure the "golden goose" continues to lay golden eggs, as everyone benefits. Therefore, those shareholders running the business need to have the authority to make operational decisions without feeling handcuffed by needing to vote on decision after decision, which is a recipe for disaster. Another priority is to protect the minority shareholders and give them a "parachute" to be able to get out—should the partnership with their family members not work out.

How do you accomplish both priorities? If the family business is a car or truck dealership, the manufacturers will require that one person have control over all decisions regarding operations. That is obviously not the case in other industries, but still there needs to be a structure allowing for business decisions to be made expediently.

The CEO of the company needs to be able to make decisions affecting daily operations, with the exception of "Issues of Major Importance." This would involve decisions made at the board of directors level, such as the ability to sell the company, sales or acquisitions in excess of a predetermined number, taking on debt outside of normal operations such as flooring costs, pay plans of executives and family members, amending shareholder or operating agreements.

Shareholder agreements should be in place, dictating what happens in the event of death, disability, termination of employment, and retirement. These agreements would also address the path whereby a shareholder can elect to be bought out, so shareholders don't feel trapped if the business relationship is not working. Again, should a shareholder elect to be bought out, the business needs plenty of runway to be able to make the payments, preventing the business from being financially obligated during a difficult market. These planning steps need to involve an attorney experienced in dealing with family business corporate structuring.

Can active and inactive shareholders coexist without damaging the business and/or family relationships? It's possible, but not recommended. Unfortunately, the priorities and perspectives of active and inactive shareholders are usually different, creating many challenging family dynamics.

I hear conversations regularly like the ones below:

*"Why aren't we making distributions to shareholders? You just said we made lots of money!"*

> **Unfortunately, the priorities and perspectives of active and inactive shareholders are usually different, creating many challenging family dynamics.**

*"Because we don't have the cash!"* or *"We need to save money for future acquisitions."*

*"But I need money now. I'm remodeling my house because you bragged to me that the company had a great year!"*

More frustrating comments between siblings sound like this:

*"Dad always gave all shareholders demos. What's the deal?"*

*"What do you mean I have to sign on the personal guarantees?"*

In a perfect world those active in the business would own the stock, and the inactive family members would inherit other assets. That would prevent much of the friction described above. But each family situation is different, and family expectations have often been developed over decades. One size does not fit all when it comes to planning. Finding solutions that take into consideration all parties is critical if the family and business are to be preserved.

Loyd Rawls, founder of The Rawls Group, likes to say, "Agreements are meant to preclude disagreements." Make sure you develop the documentation needed now before something happens to create disagreements.

It's important to remember that decisions made at one generational level may work but become significant challenges at the next generational level. Make sure your legal agreements take into consideration the impact decisions will have on the next generation. "That's the way we've always done it" is a recipe for future family and business explosions.

## WILL YOUR SIBLING CHOOSE YOU?

"Are you the person your sibling will want to be his partner?" I asked a young man planning to enter the family business that his brother had been working in for seven years. "I think so, because we have a lot of complementary skill sets that should make us great assets to each other and our family business." That's a great place to start, but the same things that complement each other can become sources of irritation.

> **In order to be effective and long-lasting, partnerships depend on you choosing your partner and him/her choosing you!**

What does it take to make a family business partnership work? In order to be effective and long-lasting, partnerships depend on you *choosing* your partner and him/her *choosing* you! This is true whether in a business partnership, a family business partnership, or a marriage. I chose my wife, and Lisa chose me—and we continue to make that choice over and over again. The same is true in your business. But family business partnerships are especially challenging because at least initially your parents created your sibling partnership. That's great if you agree, but not so great if you don't.

It's been said that "opposites attract," and there must be some truth to that old saying since most married couples I know have complementary personalities. You probably have similar values, faith, and goals, but you likely communicate differently. Generally, people choose someone as a spouse who makes them a better person and vice versa.

It's been my experience that siblings brought together as partners in family businesses often have complementary skill sets. If they can focus on each other's strengths, they can become a high-powered productive partnership. So, what's the problem?

"This was always going to be *my* business. I've been here five years. What's my sister doing changing her mind and coming into my business?" The fight was on, and the expectation was that there could be only one winner. *Wrong!* I began by asking both siblings what was important to them, which included the opportunity to grow the family business while also wanting to have families of their own. Work-life balance was important. In fact, the family business had multiple opportunities for both siblings. "Compete with other businesses, not each other" was my message. "Your focus needs to be on helping each other be successful so you can have the kind of powerful partnership that provides leadership, resulting in growth for your company." While it's easy to say, "Don't compete with your sister," it's tough to do consistently, especially when dealing with highly motivated, competitive people.

"Hell, yes, I want my brother to be my partner!" responded another business owner client. Ideally you would be able to say this about your sibling partner. What must happen if your sibling partnership is currently challenged, but you want it to work?

Two brothers committed to having a productive, positive, fun partnership reached out to me to work on building that kind of structure and defusing any potential land mines before they blew up their family and business. One brother had been involved in the family business for almost ten years, and his brother had been working there for less than one year. Fortunately, they both realized their complementary skill sets could create a dynamic partnership if they didn't screw it up.

We began by examining how they are different. One brother is very organized, structured, strategic, but not people focused. His brother is a people person, who immediately ingratiates himself to those people working with him. Identifying areas where they could clash and/or misinterpret each other's actions or intents and how they can complement each other was important to this process of building their partnership.

> Identifying the expectations each brother has of the other and what they expect of themselves in regard to meeting the partnership needs was an important step.

Identifying the expectations each brother has of the other and what they expect of themselves in regard to meeting the partnership needs was an important step. Putting this on paper was key, and then we discussed what each meant to minimize assumptions. I reminded them, "You are different, so what you mean by saying, 'I will communicate my opinions thoughtfully,' may be very different from what your brother hears."

I emphasized to the brothers that a weekly meeting is sacred time between the two of you! If the two of you are going to someday lead the company, then there is no more important meeting you can have. Block your calls, get away from distractions, and let others know how important this hour is to you. Making sure you come to this meeting with an agenda of business issues to discuss with your partner is a sign you value this time and its importance in building the type of partnership you want.

These two brothers recognized that *together* they can do great things, sharing the burdens and the victories. Both are highly talented, committed, focused, competitive men wanting to grow their business and impact their community. I have no doubt they will be a force for their competitors to contend with in the years to come.

**If your partnership is going to work, you must work at it.**

If your partnership is going to work, you must work at it. Effective partnerships take time and effort to build trust, whether it's your marriage partnership, a business partnership, or a family business sibling partnership. The main question you have to ask yourself is "Am I the person my sibling will say, 'Absolutely, I *choose you* to be my partner'?"

## FAMILY PARTNERSHIPS THAT WORK

Most business owners would say that there can be only one boss. In the case of our auto dealer clients, their manufacturers will accept only one person as the leader. But in the forty-plus years I've worked with family business owners, I've seen many sibling partnerships effectively operating as fifty-fifty partners, even if the actual stock ownership is not fifty-fifty. How does that work?

"You and your brother are extremely strong, opinionated leaders who often argue like crazy over your differences of opinion, yet you've been effective running your businesses together for over thirty-five years. To what do you attribute your successful partnership?" I asked two sixty-plus-year-old brothers.

They responded: "We agreed a long time ago that we can argue our individual positions as hard as we want in private, but once we make a decision, it becomes *our* decision. We never say, 'I told you so.' If the decision is a good one, *we* celebrate together, and if it is a bad decision, *we* fix it together."

What do family partnerships have in common where two siblings are working together in concert for the good of the business? Consider the responses of other successful sibling partnerships:

*"My brother and I decided a long time ago to divide up our responsibilities based on what we each like and do best."*

*"When making decisions we try to collaborate, but if we disagree, we tend to lean in the direction of the one of us most involved in the area of responsibility."*

*"We recognized a long time ago that it's lonely at the top if you have to go it alone. Having my sibling as my partner means we can carry each other's load, and we definitely have each other's back."*

*"We understand that our manufacturers will only accept someone having the final vote—so in our agreement, with some manufacturers my sister is the designated majority vote, and with other manufacturers I'm the majority vote."*

> **They are not competing with each other; rather they are collaborating for the good of their family business and competing with the outside world.**

What's the common thread among these partnerships, which involve brothers and sisters in their fifties, sixties, and seventies? They are not competing *with* each other; rather they are collaborating for the good of their family business and competing with the outside world.

Each of these strong leaders recognizes that there is strength in numbers and that two are better than one. Utilizing their complementary strengths and skills, they have forged a leadership team that allows them to grow their business. This involves dividing the tasks and responsibilities and, at the same time, working together to make the higher-level decisions.

The key word is *collaborating*, which involves a lot of work (hence *co-laboring*). It's no different than in a marriage, which is definitely a form of partnership and clearly one in which, if you want it to be a strong, positive, impactful relationship, you must be willing to work at it.

For this type of partnership to work, there must be a high level of trust and respect. You must be the type of person who your sibling needs and wants. The presumption is that you are *both* contributing significantly to the partnership. This doesn't mean you must contribute equally, because it is understood you are different and bring complementary skill sets that benefit the whole.

"I feel like I'm being taken advantage of by my sister, who doesn't work nearly as many hours as I do," said the frustrated sibling partner. This remark was made by a young client who is trying to make her relationship work with her sibling but is struggling with one of the common time bombs that make family partnerships challenging. Building your partnership doesn't mean the absence of conflict—it means being willing to work through conflict.

**Building your partnership doesn't mean the absence of conflict—it means being willing to work through conflict.**

I am walking a fine line here, but it must be understood that one partner can't rely on the other to do the majority of the heavy lifting, under the guise of "You're better suited to do those things," resulting in one working more and carrying more of the business burdens. On the other hand, a baseball team needs a pitcher and a catcher, not two pitchers, so your sibling will likely be charged with responsibilities that are different from yours.

Especially when siblings are young and partnerships are being formed to run the business after the parents retire or die, each sibling may spend time doing certain jobs that require more or less hours. Note to self: You can't keep score (and neither can your spouse), otherwise your dream partnership won't work!

Do you want to have more "work-life balance"? Invest time in making your sibling partnership work. Do you want to have more fun and less stress running your business? Invest effort in making your sibling partnership work. Do you want to have someone you can confide in that you trust to have your back at all times? Invest labor in making your sibling partnership work.

Why?

*"Because my sibling is my best friend, and together we make an unbeatable team."*

*"Because we share a bond of trust that is powerful when making business decisions."*

*"Because we share the responsibilities, lightening the load for each of us and bringing greater strength of leadership to our company."*

While I've never been in a sibling partnership, I've been in several partnerships and have experienced the good, the bad, and the ugly. I understand how tough it is to make this relationship work for the benefit of both partners. Jeff Bannon is thirty years younger than I am, yet we make decisions as coequals and work to support each other's success. I am also a partner at The Rawls Group, where our culture is one of "What can I do to help you and cheer for you?"

Partnerships admittedly aren't for everyone, but for many, "Isn't this what you want?"

# 6

# **Blended Families**

"What do you mean my child
isn't getting promoted?"

# Time Bomb #6

# *Blended Families*

## BLENDED FAMILIES: CHALLENGING IN THE FAMILY BUSINESS

This is a very personal subject for me, because I am divorced and my family has experienced firsthand the challenges of navigating a blended family. Divorce is painful and unfortunately very common in our society, so many families understand the struggles up close and personal. There are no winners in a divorce, just survivors, and hopefully if you're among the survivors, your family has experienced forgiveness and healing, making the best of a difficult situation. In the environment of a family business, blended family challenges can feel like challenges on steroids.

> "What's Dad going to do with the business stock? Will we have to contend with his new wife owning a piece?"

"What's Dad going to do with the business stock? Will we

have to contend with his new wife owning a piece?" The fact that this is on the minds of the business owner's children is divisive at best. If the children believe Dad will include his new wife in stock ownership, they now have a potential threat to their succession expectations. She becomes the villain in the story, but it doesn't have to be that way.

The solution involves Dad developing a plan to provide for his new wife with assets separate from the business. The business owner's children expect their father to provide for his wife, but their fear is that the plan will involve business assets, including stock and real estate, that they expected to ultimately be theirs. The separation of assets between the owner's new wife and his children needs to be a high priority.

In an initial conversation with a new business owner client, he remarked that his second wife had given him the impression that she would like to work with his children in the business should something happen to him. She had worked in the business for several years prior to their marriage. Clearly, this was an awkward conversation, and as such, the business owner had not pursued it further.

Knowing I had to clarify what she was expecting, I made the following remark to his wife over dinner with the two of them that night. "Your husband definitely wants to provide for you and fortunately has multiple businesses. How many stores would you like? The only thing we can't do is set up a plan for you and his children to be in business together—that won't work." Fortunately, her response was that she had no intention of working in his business and would not want stock ownership. You could hear my client's sigh of relief from a mile away. Sometimes it's just a matter of getting tough subjects out in the open for discussion.

Since this was a potentially confrontational subject, he had understandably avoided it but was worried it was something his wife wanted. He had been concerned about this for some time and didn't know how to solve it. Unfortunately, communication in the best of situations is often unsatisfactory. This is a perfect example of the tension created in blended family situations, especially when involving family business assets. Wouldn't it be nice if every challenging blended family problem was solvable?

The challenge in family business is always balancing between focusing on "family first" or "business first." When there is a blended family, it appears more complicated. In making decisions, it is important to ask, "How will my decision affect my business (since it produces the golden eggs that provide for everyone)?" When addressing issues regarding the family and their involvement with your business, it is important to ask yourself if you would make the same decision if the person were not family.

> **The challenge in family business is always balancing between focusing on "family first" or "business first."**

For instance, there are differences of opinion as to whether to allow in-laws to be involved and work in the family business. Some owners say a definite "no way," fearing this just complicates things. Plus, "What if my daughter and her husband get a divorce?" No doubt that would create challenges. On the other hand, I can cite numerous examples in which the son-in-law became the successor, leading the company successfully. As a result, in one client situation, the grandchildren are now following their father (the son-in-law), and the expectation among the family is that the family business legacy is alive and well.

"A prenuptial agreement is a requirement if my child wants to inherit stock!" exclaimed one business owner. Almost every business owner worries that his/her child will experience a divorce, and the odds are high this could happen. As a result, this conversation becomes part of most business succession planning. When addressing a prenuptial, you will need to work with an attorney experienced in marital law. Most important to remember is a prenuptial agreement must be addressed long before the wedding (as opposed to a week or two before, which I've seen several times). If you wait until the last minute, you risk the negativity that often surrounds a prenuptial dominating the relationship, making a divorce more likely to happen.

> **A Family Business Employment Policy should be developed in writing.**

"What do I do when my stepchildren want to be involved in my business?" There is definitely no easy answer, and one size does not fit all in these situations. Again, the primary question to ask is "Would I hire my stepchild if he/she were not related to me?"

This can become very personal and emotional between you and your spouse if you have not addressed this issue long before it happens. A Family Business Employment Policy should be developed in writing, which spells out what is required for someone from your family to be hired. Educational requirements, work experience, and the application process (the same as for any non-family member) are just some of the requirements stated in your Family Business Employment Policy.

Then when the inevitable response to a child being turned down for a job is "Why didn't you hire my son? You hired your daughter!" you can point to objective reasons, such as "He hasn't met the education requirement" or "He got fired from his last job, and our policy says we only hire family members with a positive prior work experience."

Blended families often come with a host of emotions, guilt,

regrets, and walking on eggshells when interacting because of the hurt and damage to relationships. When this combustible combination is injected into a family business environment, decisions are frequently made that are not in the best interests of the family or business.

**And, by the way, prayer is super important!**

To overcome these challenges, it is important for families to work at communicating, trying hard to understand where each family member is coming from, applying forgiveness and understanding, and giving each other the benefit of the doubt. And, by the way, prayer is super important!

## "I'VE GOT A PROBLEM: 40 Percent TO THE IRS, 50 Percent TO MY SECOND WIFE, 50 Percent TO MY CHILDREN?"

You're correct if your math tells you that is one too many large percentages. For the family business owner attempting to resolve his business succession and estate plan, this can be a giant problem.

How does this problem evolve? If you are married for a second time (or more) and do not have a properly drafted and executed prenuptial or postmarital agreement, you could be headed for a planning nightmare in many states under the augmented estate/ elective share rules.

Let me set the possible scene for you. Ben Business Owner had been married for thirty years when his wife dies. Two of his three children are active in his business and expect to continue the family legacy. Ben gets remarried several years later. A prenuptial agreement sounds like you are on your way to divorce court, so Ben is reluctant to force his new wife, Sara, to sign one. And Ben figures this is a lifetime commitment, so it shouldn't make any difference; he expects to take care of his new wife. With his net worth, there are ample assets to provide for Sara without impacting the family businesses—or so Ben thinks.

So, what's the problem? In many states, under the augmented estate/elective share rules, Sara will become entitled to 50 percent of Ben and Sara's combined estates after only ten years of marriage (the number of years varies depending on the state). Since Sara's net worth is minimal, this means Sara becomes heir by law to approximately 50 percent of Ben's estate (regardless of when Ben acquired the assets).

> Those children active in the business will probably end up in business with Sara (it's rarely a good situation for a stepmom and stepchildren to be financially intertwined) or be facing significant payments to buy her out.

What are Ben's children facing? Let's say Ben is worth $50 million, of which his business represents $20 million. Assume Ben and Sara are married for ten-plus years at the time of his death. His estate will owe $25 million to Sara and approximately $9 million in estate taxes to the IRS (assuming the federal estate tax exemption is still at $13.61 million per person and the tax rate is 40 percent). That leaves only $16 million (not even the value of the business) to divide between his three children, two of which want to continue the business. There just aren't enough assets to go around.

Those children active in the business will probably end up in business with Sara (it's rarely a good situation for a stepmom and stepchildren to be financially intertwined) or be facing significant payments to buy her out. The plan positions Sara on the side of the IRS since she will be motivated to argue for the business and all other assets to be valued as high as possible, due to her receiving

50 percent of their value. Clearly, this places her in an adversarial relationship with the rest of the family.

The business is the golden goose, so it will also have to shoulder the burden of paying the estate taxes. In addition, how do you provide for the one child who is not active in the business? Remember, the 40 percent due in federal taxes (hopefully this situation doesn't take place in a state with inheritance taxes on top of the federal estate taxes, such as New York or Oregon, to name a couple) and the 50 percent obligation to Ben's second wife have wiped out most of the assets Ben expected his children would receive. Not enough assets means the active and inactive children will be forced to share the business assets, and this often leads to more trouble. Bottom line: too many obligations placed on the back of the business may wipe out its economic viability or even bankrupt the company.

**As awkward as it is to ask for a prenuptial agreement, this step is essential to protecting your family and business.**

How do you avoid this devastating problem? The key is to have a proper prenuptial agreement. Ben didn't intend to give his second wife of only ten years 50 percent of everything he's earned over a lifetime. Therefore, as awkward as it is to ask for a prenuptial agreement, this step is essential to protecting your family and business.

What is needed? Disclosure and representation. Both Ben and Sara need to be represented by separate attorneys in this prenuptial process, and they each need to fully disclose their net worth if there is to be any chance that the prenuptial will hold up in the future. In addition, most states require the agreement to be signed in advance of the wedding—the sooner, the better.

Not to be forgotten is the fact that second marriages are not immune from divorce. So how do the augmented estate/elective share rules come into play in a divorce settlement? Again, I'm not an attorney, and you will need to seek legal counsel to determine the impact, if any, in your state. But I am familiar with a situation in which my client had to pay a higher percentage of his estate to his ex-wife because of the threat of the augmented estate/elective share rule. While he had a prenuptial, it had been done at the last minute without full disclosure, and his attorneys believed the prenuptial would not protect him against the augmented estate/elective share rule.

> All too often business owners, when focused on getting married, do not seek knowledgeable legal advice.

It is imperative that legal counsel be sought by anyone wanting to understand the legal ramifications of this problem in their state. Not every state has these rules, and it varies from state to state. Having worked exclusively with family business owners throughout the country for many years, I am convinced that all too often business owners, when focused on getting married, do not seek knowledgeable legal advice. As a result, unknowingly they do not protect their estate, and this results in significant family, estate, and business succession problems. The only winners in that game will be the IRS and the attorneys.

## "HENRY (FORD) WOULDN'T HAVE WANTED IT THIS WAY"

This quote from the *Wall Street Journal* in the August 29, 1988 issue titled "Even the Estate of Henry Ford Causes Controversy" focused on just one of many planning problems that can develop when there are second (or third) marriages involved. What was the problem? Could Henry Ford's problem be your problem?

It appears that Henry was advised he could avoid all estate taxes at his death by putting all assets into a trust for the benefit of his wife. At her subsequent death, the estate taxes would be due, but since she was only forty-eight and Henry was seventy at the time of his death, this deferral of tax would probably involve twenty-five to thirty years or more. What a great idea! Defer $175 million of estate taxes for potentially thirty years. By factoring use of money, the tax savings are phenomenal.

So, what is the problem? To avoid estate taxes, this trust required that there be only one beneficiary: Henry's wife. She would have to die for Henry's children to receive their inheritance. Since they were all in their forties, it was quite conceivable that their stepmother would outlive them, thereby negating any inheritance. At the very least, Henry's children would not receive their inheritance until they were in their seventies or eighties. This sounds like material for the latest television hit series *Yellowstone* or *Succession*. Is it any wonder this made the front page of the *WSJ* and Henry's family ended up in court?

How could this happen? Obviously, Henry had access to many of the finest attorneys money could buy, and I certainly was not privy to what Henry intended. However, it is very possible that Henry was focused only on tax savings and missed the consequences this would have on his children.

Ironically, many business owners reading this book have this same type of trust for the benefit of their spouse and the protection of their family. Did you make a mistake? Probably not, if your wife is the mother of your children. However, even in this "same wife and mother" scenario, you need to consider the issue of *when* you want your children to receive any of their inheritance. But . . . if you have a "second wife planning situation," a red flag should go up if you are considering the use of a trust to avoid estate taxes at your death.

What about the business owner who wants his children to continue his legacy via the succession of his business? Couldn't this trust planning provide assets to be placed in a trust for his second wife and children, thus avoiding estate taxes? The answer is no for several practical reasons.

> If you have a "second wife planning situation," a red flag should go up if you are considering the use of a trust to avoid estate taxes at your death.

Pragmatically, in the real world, business is usually cyclical. Business owners often need to loan their business significant sums of money to help out in the down times. If estate tax is to be avoided, this would not be possible. Also, after the owner is gone, it is a highly unusual situation when the second wife has the same agenda as the business owner's children. Your children and your second wife usually should not share in common ownership of assets, even in a trust—especially if the succession of your business is your objective.

Avoiding tax after the death of the owner will not always work, especially when there is a second marriage. Obviously, you want to provide for your wife, but your plan should enable these assets to be separate from the business; otherwise, trouble and conflict are just around the corner.

Bottom line: for any estate and family business succession plan to be successful, it must deal with the issue of how to pay the estate taxes. Recognizing the impact taxes will have on the availability of assets to provide for your second wife and children is key. Don't cop out here. "The kids will have to solve the problem after I'm gone" involves kicking the can down the road, leading to disaster. You and you alone must make the hard decisions.

"Henry wouldn't have wanted it this way"—and neither would you. Henry Ford's estate plan was legally perfect yet created a financial and family nightmare. Consult competent advisers and make sure your plan creates harmony and *succession*, not *WSJ* headlines.

## FAMILIES COME IN DIFFERENT SHAPES AND SIZES

Can cousins work together? How about in-laws? Some say "no way" while others have responded very positively. What makes the difference? Family businesses often start with one founder, but as they progress from generation to generation, many other family combinations come into play.

Among several family businesses that I have worked with, each evolved in a different manner. The founder of the first company passed the business to his two sons and daughter, who then passed the business to a daughter and son-in-law and another son. The founder of the second company passed the business to his two sons, who then passed it to their two sons (cousins). The founder of the third company passed the business to a daughter and son-in-law, who then passed the business to two daughters. The founder of the fourth company passed the business to his daughter and son-in-law, who then passed the business to their daughter and son-in-law, who then passed the business to their daughter and son-in-law, who then passed the business to their son and

**Families come in lots of shapes and sizes, and I've witnessed all types of family variations experiencing success.**

daughter, whose husband runs the business with his brother-in-law. *Are you confused?* Families come in lots of shapes and sizes, and I've witnessed all types of family variations experiencing success.

One client that I've worked with for over twenty-five years is now being run by Generation 5 and is planning for Generation 6. Generation 5 is made up of six cousins from two families. Not only have they figured out how to work together, but they've far surpassed the business profitability experienced by their fathers.

Another family business I've worked with for over thirty years has two Generation 4 cousins who have successfully led their company for twelve years and have tripled the business profitability of their Generation 3 fathers.

A third family business that I've worked with for fifteen years involves multiple brothers who are in the process of transitioning their business to their children. As cousins, they are working through the issues and building a structure that will allow them to succeed together.

## Why does it work for some families and not for others?

These are just some examples of different variations of families overcoming challenges and finding ways to work together to continue their family business legacy.

Why does it work for some families and not for others? No matter whether you are dealing with cousins, in-laws, brothers, sisters, or any combination, succession only works when the players understand that each one must be the person the others want to be in business with, not just because they are related.

Do you have the work ethic, drive, and attitude that draw people to you as well as, the leadership abilities and the commitment? Do your partners like you? Are you a team player who helps others succeed? Will people follow your leadership? When you can answer these questions affirmatively, then it doesn't matter whether you're my sister or cousin or in-law. We can work together and help our family business succeed.

You may have been brought together by the previous generation because you are related in some way, but for this next generation to succeed together, you must believe in each other and know your partners have the best interests of the business in mind.

Unfortunately, I've also seen too many situations where the next generation is facing very difficult challenges. Cousins feel trapped with future family partners who are not as committed nor do they share the same work ethic. Unfortunately, the uncles did not raise their children the same, with one allowing entitlement issues to dominate. This won't work in the long run, and the fathers will need to bring accountability into play and hope for some maturing; more likely, they will need one family to buy out the other or else sell the whole company.

Can any of these challenges be overcome? Yes, but the sooner you deal with them, the better. My partners and I are involved regularly with younger generations, helping them understand their differences and what they need to do to be able to work together, and then working with them as they practice the steps that need to be taken to overcome their partnership challenges. Accountability needs to be practiced daily, and usually the older generation needs to be involved in this process. Let's face it—the older generation created a lot of the mess we are dealing with.

"What if my daughter and son-in-law get a divorce?" This fear and the knowledge that divorce is all too common often result in business owners deciding they don't want to take that risk by bringing the in-law into their business. But I've been privileged to work with many sons-in-law who have done a great job for years and years, fully committed to their family and the business. There are no guarantees, but many business owners with whom I've worked praise their in-law for the great job they've done leading the family business into the future.

Family business succeeds when family members, regardless of their relationship to each other, commit themselves to the success of the company. You can't change anyone but yourself, so if you're in business with other family members, are you the person they want to be their partner?

# 7

# Reading of the Will

"Surprise!"

# Time Bomb #7

# Estate Planning Mistakes = Business Nightmares

## WHAT YOUR FAMILY DOESN'T KNOW MAY HURT THEM

An estate and family business succession plan can often be a ticking time bomb waiting to explode. It's a sensitive subject loaded with pyrotechnic emotions, which often lead to hurt feelings, family divisiveness, destructive relationships, and the loss of a dream—the owner's family continuing his legacy. These problems can be avoided.

A few years ago I was asked by the CEO son of a manufacturing company to meet with his parents regarding their estate and family business succession planning. I asked if he was concerned about what he knew or what he didn't know regarding their planning. He said, "Both!" Since he had invested over twenty-five years in the business, he wanted to know what had been decided regarding the business and what obligations he would be responsible for regarding his siblings.

Upon meeting the parents, I discovered that a lot of excellent planning had been done. Mom and Dad's response was, "It's all been handled—we don't have any problems."

"Yes and no" was my response. I agreed that most of the planning was very well done—but without the decisions being properly communicated to their children, the seeds for disaster were being sown.

As the parent, your reasons for making these decisions affecting your children may make perfect sense—and the decisions are rightfully yours to make. But, if your children are not informed ahead of your passing, they may come to very different conclusions as to why you decided things—"Obviously Mom and Dad didn't love me as much as my siblings." That's not the message you want them to remember you by.

> **Without the decisions being properly communicated to their children, the seeds for disaster were being sown.**

After the death of a business owner, his son called asking for help dealing with his siblings. "We are all very emotional, feeling very vulnerable, and it is definitely affecting our relationships as we try to work together to settle his estate." One of the challenges was their father's unwillingness to communicate his wishes directly to his children. As a result, a lot of assumptions were made about who knew what as well as what Dad had intended, resulting in the erosion of trust. Since Dad was gone, there was no way to gain closure, and this family was suffering as a result. Instead of focusing on their many reasons to be thankful, they were struggling with each other.

The problem is often perceptions and lack of understanding. Parents are usually concerned with treating all of their children fairly. *Fair* is generally defined as "equal," but when there are assets such as a business and real estate involved, equal is virtually impossible for most families.

A deceased business owner's son asked us, "Why would Dad have set up the plan that way? That's not fair!" Unfortunately, since Dad was gone, there was no way to ask him. The advisers tried to explain, but only Dad's response would be adequate—and that was no longer possible. This son perceived that he was treated unfairly, and without Dad's response, the son could only turn his anger at his siblings, who he felt had manipulated their father's final decision.

**"Why would Dad have set up the plan that way? That's not fair!"**

Bottom line: Mom and Dad should have the final say. It is their estate, and therefore they have the right to do whatever they please. *But, but, but* that only works if Mom and Dad don't care what happens after they are gone. That is not the case with the vast majority of family business owners I have known and worked with over the years. Usually when an owner says, "I don't care what happens; I'll be dead," he really means, "I don't know how to solve my problem, so I'll avoid dealing with it."

Most business owners do care about their families and want their families to be the beneficiaries of their lifetime of work. For many owners it is very important that their children have the opportunity to inherit and successfully continue the operation of their business.

For a family business succession plan to succeed, it must deal with the emotional family issues. Communication with family members is a vital ingredient, and on these sensitive issues it is often very difficult. But avoiding conflict will not prevent problems. Usually, an outside adviser, someone who understands the unique family business succession planning environment and is skilled in helping families deal with these emotional issues, is critical and can help family members to understand why certain decisions are being made.

A Family Business Council, facilitated by a trusted adviser, is an excellent way to share Mom and Dad's vision, plan, goals, and objectives. It becomes a forum where issues are clarified, questions are answered, intentions are illuminated. I recommend making this an annual event so your children can hear from you many times about why you set up your plan as you did. Communication is often challenging and people hear things they want to hear, so repetition is important when sharing your estate and business succession plans.

Mom and Dad have the final say, but it is very helpful when your children understand your motives and intentions. They may not agree, but they are more likely to accept and move forward if they have heard it directly from you. The worst option is for them to be surprised, finding out after you are gone, when there is nothing they can do. Often their frustration or anger then gets directed at their siblings. The last thing you want is for your estate and business succession plan to drive a wedge between your children.

You definitely want your family to succeed as well as your business. If family harmony is going to happen—both now and after you are gone—communication regarding business succession must take place, even if it's uncomfortable in nature.

Otherwise, you may have a ticking time bomb as did the Camp family, owners of Camp Automotive, Inc. (as reported in the July 29, 1998 issue of the *Wall Street Journal*).

With active and inactive children all owning stock, the goals and objectives of each Camp family member were differing, as one might expect. After their father's death in 1995, these pent-up emotions exploded. Their nightmare is summarized in this quote from the *WSJ*: "But before long [Phil Camp's] brothers had all but stopped speaking to him. . . . 'There is a lot of friction, anger and bitterness,' says Mr. Camp's sister, Julie Camp McKay."

Is your family and business success worth the price of communication, even when it's uncomfortable? Only you can answer this very personal question. Choosing to meet with family members *now* in an atmosphere where issues are addressed, feelings are aired, and questions are answered can prevent heartache and/or business failure later.

## GRATEFUL OR RESENTFUL: WHAT WILL YOUR ESTATE PLANNING PRODUCE?

One of the universal things parents want to hear is, "Thanks, Mom and Dad!" This is especially important when we feel we've gone above and beyond to provide something for our children and grandchildren. Knowing our children are grateful usually inspires us to want to do more for them. On the contrary, when we don't receive thanks, it has the opposite effect, creating resentment or at least frustration on our part. What does this have to do with succession and estate planning? Plenty!

Over the past year my partners and I have been constantly reminding our clients of the need to utilize their lifetime exemption since the sooner you utilize it, the greater the impact on reducing your estate taxes.

**Issues such as "How will this affect our lifestyle?" and "Will this adversely affect our children?" are critical questions that must be answered.**

As a result, there have been many client discussions regarding how to gift assets to your children. Issues such as "How will this affect our lifestyle?" and "Will this adversely affect our children?" are critical questions that must be answered. Otherwise you are not going to feel comfortable engaging in gifting millions of dollars to your children (even if it's via trusts, partnerships, or LLCs, where the children's ability to get their hands on the money is minimal).

When gifts are made, often the parents desire to "treat each of our children fairly." Therefore, "If I'm going to give a gift to one child, I need to gift a similar amount to my other children." In most client situations, one or more of the children are active in the business but the rest are not involved. This often leads to discussions regarding gifting business stock to the active children and real estate or other assets to those not involved. The most important question you should consider when gifting is "Will the asset be *meaningful* to my child?" *Meaningful* usually is defined as "income producing."

To those active in the business, receiving stock means they have the opportunity to grow the business and usually will receive compensation accordingly (salary, bonuses, dividends, distributions from S corp stock, or their interest in LLCs). Therefore, receiving stock is very meaningful. But if you are not making distributions, stock ownership for the inactive shareholder child is nice but not meaningful—and, in fact, it can be frustrating.

> "I need it now while I'm raising children, have a mortgage, need to pay college expenses, etc."

"My brother is getting lots of money from the business, but I'm getting nothing!"

"But he works in the business, and you don't."

While that is correct, it doesn't award you the appreciation you were hoping to receive for making the gift.

Unfortunately, all too often I see business owners *only* focusing on minimizing taxes by gifting equity to get it out of their estates.

While this is very important for succession and estate planning, the impact on the children is often lost when they receive assets that are not meaningful to them.

Let me explain. When a child receives an interest in the business real estate or stock (often via an LLC or trust) but you never make distributions, inadvertently the seeds of resentment have been sown. I have witnessed many business owners' children who are told they have received an interest worth millions of dollars (the inference being that they should be grateful), but they will need to wait until the parent dies before the asset becomes meaningful, giving them income to impact lifestyle. Their thinking is "I need it now while I'm raising children, have a mortgage, need to pay college expenses, etc."

Often complicating the situation is that their sibling is working in the business and receiving all the perks afforded by this involvement, usually translated as the active child enjoying a higher standard of living than the non-involved sibling. Granted, each child made their own decision as to whether to get involved in your business. But every parent I know wants their children to have good relationships with each other. What you don't want is your children becoming resentful of their siblings. So, how do we prevent this?

*Meaningful* does not mean *equal!* While the value of assets gifted may be in the millions, *meaningful* income will usually be significantly less. For most young people raising families, $25,000, $50,000, or $100,000 is often a game changer. Therefore, if you distribute this amount from the millions of dollars gifted

**Meaningful does not mean *equal!***

to an LLC or trust, you create an atmosphere of *gratefulness*. By receiving this income, each of your children are benefiting from your generosity now, not having to wait until you are gone to enjoy the financial benefits of being in your family. Instead of focusing on the lifestyle enjoyed by their siblings active in the business, they are now hopefully focusing on the benefits they are receiving.

Unfortunately, no one can predict how any individual child will respond, and some will complain no matter what you do. But, if your planning goal is to have your family enjoy Thanksgiving together with loving family relationships, then any planning you do should consider what is *meaningful* to each family member. Grateful or resentful? Clearly, we all want to hear, "Thanks, Mom and Dad!"

## WHY EQUAL IS NOT FAIR, AND FAIR IS NOT EQUAL

"But I love all my kids equally, and I want to treat them fairly," exclaimed Ted (not his real name), the exasperated business owner who was trying to figure out his estate plan. This sentiment is voiced over and over by my family business owner clients, leading to many discussions on "why equal is not fair."

It's easy to relate to this concern as most of us have experienced what I call "the Christmas/Hanukkah Syndrome." This happens as you lay out your children's gifts on your bed or table and start figuring out whether you have bought the right number of gifts for each one. "Let's see, I have three gifts for John and only two for Hannah, but the two for Hannah cost more than the three for John. How do I make this work?" When we apply the same thinking to our estate planning, it can really get crazy.

I believe it is important to remember that when your children were growing up, you didn't say, "I just paid $5,000 for braces for Ken; therefore, I need to spend $5,000 on each of my other kids." Clearly, you spent money on braces for Ken because they were needed—and you would do the same for your other children depending on their needs.

Most business owners hire a succession planner to help them keep the business in the family. Their goal is to perpetuate their family business legacy and address the myriad of interrelated and interconnected issues involved in making their dream come true. Often the business owner has multiple children, and only one or two are active in their business. The big question they face is how to make their business succession goal happen while providing an estate distribution plan that treats all their children equally or fairly (often defined by business owners and their spouses as one and the same).

What's involved in making sure your successor children will have the resources to continue successfully running your business after you are gone? *Cash and assets!* While you might have started with nothing and committed all your assets to buying and building your business, today you have the luxury of access to all your assets to provide the resources necessary to be able to run your business. In 2009 and 2010, that was critical to your survival. Banks weren't lending, and you probably had to scramble to find the cash necessary to simply pay your bills. Those business owners with cash were also able to take advantage of the market conditions, and as opportunities became available (often due to other business owners going broke), owners with cash bought businesses at bargain prices. Cash and a strong balance sheet are always keys to success.

Real estate is also an essential part of most successful family businesses I've been involved with. This requires a significant commitment of cash to purchase and inevitably be able to respond when upgrades are demanded. Real estate is also a wonderful source of capital; you can borrow against the equity when your situation requires capital.

In a perfect world, your estate plan would designate all the business stock and real estate for your children who are active in your business. Unfortunately, most family business owners have built their net worth by reinvesting in their business, so their business represents the majority of their assets. If you have children who are not active in your business, this can present real problems.

Recently I met with the successor son of a business owner; several siblings in the family are not active in the business, and the son said, "I just hope my father will take into consideration the large increase in the net worth of this business since I've been involved in running it." He recognizes that his parents will want to provide for his siblings, but he is worried about how much he will have to pay in order to make this happen. "Will it be fair?" is what he is asking.

**"Will it be fair?" is what he is asking.**

His younger sister is also asking, "Will it be fair?" as she is concerned that her age will mean she doesn't get the same opportunity as her older brother. "Why should I get less than him, just because he started a few years ahead of me? I am significantly contributing to the success of the business!" She is saying she wants the stock divided equally, but her brother would respond, "That's not fair. I've put in years more and should receive more stock—equal is not fair!"

So, what is the solution? There isn't just one. First, recognize that the only way to be equal is either to have one child (too late for most of us) or to sell everything and turn it all into cash, which can be divided equally. Obviously, you're not going to do that if you want to have a succession plan for your business.

Start by looking at your assets in terms of answering this question: "Is this asset meaningful to my child who will be receiving it?" *Meaningful* is usually defined as "income producing." If I am running the business, then I can create income for myself. If I am a minority shareholder, then I am at the mercy of the majority owner as to whether there will be any distributions. (Worst case, I have taxable income due to my minority interest, but no distributions are made for me to be able to pay my income taxes!)

It has been my experience that when each of your children receives income-producing assets, which they can use to improve their lifestyle, they are not as concerned if the shares they each receive are equal.

*Is family harmony important?* If your answer is yes, don't put your children in a position of having to share the same assets. Not many people can share the same sandbox without fighting! Everyone inevitably has their own perspective of what is fair. Solutions probably won't happen overnight as you may need to have those active in the business buying out those who aren't employed by the business over time or buying life insurance for your inactive children to create some equality. If you decide to have inactive shareholders, you will need to establish detailed governance as to how this will work and what each family member can expect.

> **Equal is not fair. Perspective is everything.**

Setting expectations in advance is a very important way to prevent your children from being at odds with each other after you are gone. If your children hear your plan directly from you (possibly with the help of your advisers), they will be inclined to accept it, knowing it was your decision to make. The last thing you want is for your wonderful business to destroy your family. Equal is not fair. Perspective is everything.

# 8

# Passing the Baton

"Dad says that I'm his successor but
when's he going to let go?!?"

# Time Bomb #8

# *Passing the Baton Challenges*

## "I DON'T WANT TO RETIRE"

I've heard this a thousand times from business owner clients over the forty-plus years I've been a business succession planner. I understand—I don't want to retire, and I'm nine years older than my father was when he retired. For most business owners, you love what you do, and you probably feel like Bobby Bowden, the FSU football coach, who was reported to say, "I don't want to retire and die six months later like Bear Bryant!" To many, retirement feels like the end.

"I want a succession plan to continue my life's work." This is the primary reason why business owners hire me and my partners at The Rawls Group. As succession planners, developing a succession plan and dealing with an owner who doesn't want to retire creates a giant challenge. Succession demands change, and the options include a seamless transition, a long and painful process, or even a potential explosion, resulting in the destruction of your business.

Your actions and attitude as the owner will play a large role in determining what happens.

For your succession plan to work, your successor(s) must be ready to go, fully prepared to take over the leadership of the company. For succession to be seamless, the successor must have demonstrated his/her competency, and that means the current owner must provide an atmosphere in which the successor(s) can gain leadership experience and demonstrate they will be able to lead the company. There should be no doubt in any of the management team's minds that the successor(s) are capable, respected, and will successfully be able to lead the company into the future.

In a recent article "Developing an Exit Strategy . . . or Not," written by my partner Jeff Faulkner, he stated, "One of the most significant factors negatively impacting effective succession plans is business owners who do not leave." [Jeff Faulkner, "Developing an Exit Strategy . . . or Not," Rawls, "https://seekingsuccession.com/exit-strategy-or-not/.] I agree. So, how do we prepare the successor and seamlessly transfer leadership if the owner doesn't plan on retiring or leaving the business? If you don't want to retire and you want your business legacy to continue, you are the key to making this happen.

Loyd Rawls, the founder of The Rawls Group, has been committed to succession planning for over fifty years. Better than anyone, Loyd knew that he would need to make changes in his role if Succession Success™ for The Rawls Group was going to happen. But knowing what to do and being willing to do it can be two different things. To his credit, Loyd was willing and continues to be willing to do what is necessary to ensure the ongoing Succession Success™ of our company.

To make sure his life's work would continue, Loyd committed himself to the following:

- Transfer day-to-day decision-making authority to your successor.
- Support your successor's decisions publicly. (If you disagree, do so privately.)
- Redefine your role and that of your successor.
- Meet regularly with your successor to discuss the transition and how you and your successor are doing in making this happen seamlessly—communicate, communicate, communicate.
- Accept that you and your successor are human and will step on each other's toes as you attempt to transition the company's leadership for succession. Mistakes will be made by all parties, requiring forgiveness and extending the benefit of the doubt to each other.

I'm like so many of you—retirement is not a goal of mine. But, just like Loyd, I understand that if I want my clients to continue to be well served beyond me, I need to prepare my successor(s). Therefore, I am attempting to do the following:

- Determine what part of our business I really enjoy and where I continue to add value.
- Encourage my successor(s) to take the lead in our dealings with clients. As long as I continue to add value, I don't have to worry whether clients or my successor(s) will want me to stay involved.

That's exactly what Loyd did. He loves working with clients, so he transferred the leadership and running of the company to Dave Ciambella and focused on what he is so very gifted at doing—serving the needs of his clients. He's as committed as ever and continues to play an extremely important role in our company.

As a result, Loyd and I continue to stay involved, we are still doing the parts of the business we enjoy most, and our successors want us to stay. Hopefully we all *win*! Unfortunately, as humans we often have better intentions than performance. So, I need to continuously remind myself: Attitude is everything. Unsolicited advice is dictating, and often received as from a "dictator." If you encourage, affirm, and support rather than criticize and rebuke, you are much more likely to see your successor(s) coming to you for advice and counsel, wanting you to stay.

> What's your succession role if you want your legacy to continue? Offer wise counsel, be a sounding board, a source of wisdom and experience, a chairman, and maybe even a cheerleader.

What's your succession role if you want your legacy to continue? Offer wise counsel, be a sounding board, a source of wisdom and experience, a chairman, and maybe even a cheerleader—that's how you will continue to bring value, and your successors will want you to stay. Thanks to Loyd's commitment and actions, his legacy through The Rawls Group will continue, hopefully for one hundred years.

"I don't want to retire, but I want my succession plan to work." It all depends on *you*!

## SUCCESSION SUCKS

"Succession sucks!" exclaimed our frustrated seasoned business owner client, no doubt expressing what many owners feel and have experienced. Here are a few more statements my partner Dan Iosue and I have heard over forty-plus years as succession planners working with business owner clients:

*"We sure are talking a lot about what happens if I get hit by a bus!"*

*"You're just trying to push me out of my business, and that's not going to happen!"*

*"You want me to give away my assets, just to save taxes, and I'm not comfortable with that."*

*"I don't want to ruin my kids by giving them too much too soon."*

*"This succession planning is causing me to make a lot of decisions regarding my family that I'm not comfortable making today."*

**"You're just trying to push me out of my business, and that's not going to happen!"**

Can you relate? Of course, and so can we.

Why would anyone want to go through succession planning if it means you must deal with these types of tough questions? Because *you care* about your immediate family, your extended business family, and your business, which most likely represents your life's work.

Being in control is important for most business owners. If I've learned anything working with family businesses that is universally true, it's that you want to be in control of what happens. The best way to be in control is for you to commit the time, money, and emotional expense to develop a plan that meets your objectives and then to get your plan approved by your manufacturer(s)/franchisors, if applicable.

Your plan must consider the contingencies involved in "what if I get hit by a bus tomorrow," while also anticipating an ideal timeline. This ideal timeline anticipates you becoming less dependent financially on the business over time, and the business gradually becoming less reliant upon your operational involvement. So, let's look at these concerns and see how they can be overcome.

## "We sure are talking a lot about what happens if I get hit by a bus!"

No one likes to talk about their own mortality. I spoke recently with a business owner in his seventies who sheepishly expressed that he doesn't have a will or trust. While it's hard to imagine a highly successful individual would procrastinate on such an important step in protecting his family, it is unfortunately all too common. In fact, in my experience, even when business owners have wills and trusts in place, it has been years since they reviewed these documents, and they are often woefully outdated.

One owner comes to mind, whose twenty-year-old son wasn't born at the time his will was created, so this son is referred to as an "issue" (the legal term) in the document. Not exactly what your child wants to be called!

None of us likes to deal with our own mortality, but death is one thing that will happen to all of us. Remember, this is a *when* question, not an *if* question. The mortality rate is 100 percent. None of us is getting out of here alive. So, if you want to be in control of what happens *when* it happens, make sure you have an updated will or trust in place.

## "You're just trying to push me out of my business, and that's not going to happen!"

Succession planning does not mean you need to be pushed out. However, it does mean you will need to gradually make room for your successor to be prepared to lead when you are no longer there.

Dan and I recently spent time with two eighty-plus-year-old dealers who love what they do and are not about to retire to the golf course. The great thing is that both have been able to come and go as they please for the past fifteen years because they implemented a succession plan allowing their children to eventually run the day-to-day operations in their absence. Their vision and wisdom have been irreplaceable, and they are still actively involved in providing strategic direction for their dealerships to this day. Some of the time it is at the request and encouragement of their successors. Our goal as succession planners is to develop their successors while clarifying roles, responsibilities, and expectations between the owner and successor.

### "You want me to give away my assets, just to save taxes, and I'm not comfortable with that."

Usually, the first motivation for this statement is control, which is closely followed by the need for reassurance that any asset transfer will not adversely affect your ability to maintain your lifestyle. There are many proven planning methods we utilize to accomplish your objectives so that you and your family win and the IRS loses. The IRS would love to have you continue to grow your assets, which are taxable in your estate, so that your family will have to pay 40 percent on all assets. However, there are a multitude of planning techniques that will allow you to fully retain control while transferring and/ or selling assets to reduce the size of your taxable estate. If this 40 percent estate tax rate is not addressed, it is no wonder a very small percentage of family-owned businesses continue to the next generation.

### "I don't want to ruin my kids by giving them too much too soon."

Transferring equity to your children outside your taxable estate while you remain in control allows you to determine when your children receive income from these assets. Additionally, effective communication of your plan—gifts appropriately timed (i.e., as "they earn it")—will help to ensure that your children have both earned the right to ownership of the family business and are ready once that moment arrives.

**"This succession planning is causing me to make a lot of decisions regarding my family that I'm not comfortable making today."**

This is understandable, as no one wants to cause family disharmony, and many business owners are concerned that the succession planning decisions they make will open an assortment of problems within their family.

You are the only person who is owner, operator, and parent. Therefore, you understand the issues from the standpoint of both what is necessary for the business to survive and thrive and what is fair for the family, especially the family members who are inactive in the business. Leaving this decision to your spouse, who often is ill informed as to business issues, is a recipe for disaster.

No doubt most of us can relate to one or more of these concerns. But leaders like you make tough decisions every day. There are very few decisions you will ever make that are more important than those needed to develop and implement your succession plan. Your legacy is dependent on your willingness to step up and determine what is needed for Succession Success™. Consequently, your willingness to address awkward conversations and uncomfortable decisions involved in succession planning will be one of the most rewarding returns on your investment of time and emotional energy that you will ever make.

I am grateful to my partner Dan Iosue, with whom I coauthored this content.

## CEO TO CHAIRMAN: IS IT TIME?

"I want to continue to be impactful. I don't want to become a liability to my company." Over the past year I've had numerous conversations with multiple business owners whose succession goal is to have their business continue successfully through the next generation of owners and managers. The big question is what role he/she should play, which will continue to bring value but will also prepare the company to be able to succeed when they are no longer available.

As entrepreneurs, they all share a love for their business, and most of them have no interest in retirement. But they vary in terms of how much involvement they want in the day-to-day operations of the business. One business owner said, "I do not want to follow Henry Ford's example, who went from a business icon to becoming a liability to the company in his later years." I replied that I understood he didn't want to retire, close the door, and spend his days on the golf course and playing cards. I explained that he was currently enjoying "entrepreneur's retirement," meaning "come and go as you please." He countered that wasn't exactly true, since as CEO he has responsibilities he must fulfill, and that means time commitments.

Ranging in age from fifty to eighty, these business owner clients share a common goal of seeing their family business legacy continue but differ as to what role they each want to play going forward. Each business owner has spent their adult life building their business, so they are deeply committed to the ongoing success of their company. They also each have family members who desire to succeed their elders, with various levels of experience among the next generation. Age doesn't seem to reflect their desire to stay engaged—some who want to reduce their involvement are younger.

## Succession means change, and there's the rub.

Succession means change, and there's the rub. How do you go from being 110 percent involved in everything to finding a new role that helps your successor be ready to succeed, while still allowing you to stay meaningfully engaged? Most business owners I know do not want to take the gold watch, close their door, and ride off into the sunset. Pinochle and golf seven days a week are not going to cut it for most entrepreneurs. And despite all the frustrations of being a business owner, most that I know love their business.

So where do you fit? How can you continue to positively contribute, while not becoming a liability to your company? Whether you are in your fifties or eighties, you need to answer this question: "Do I have a successor who is ready to take over tomorrow?" If the answer is yes, then you need to make sure you are at least sharing the leadership load with your successor. If the answer is no—he or she is not ready but appears to have what it takes—then you need a plan to get them ready to step in ASAP. Until your successor is ready, you need a Succession Bridge® in place to protect your company should something happen prematurely to you.

For purposes of this discussion, I'm assuming your successor is ready to lead your company today. What role should you be playing? Every one of the business owners I've referred to continues to bring wisdom, experience, historical perspective, the ability to ask critically important questions, and often vision and creativity. These qualities are priceless. These are the qualities that create the most value for your company today as well as business continuity tomorrow. These are the qualities of the Chairman of the Board.

For your company to achieve Succession Success™, you need to make room for your successor to be CEO, in charge of the daily operations of your business. Your successor needs to make the decisions you've been making so the transition of leadership is seamless, which is in the best interests of your company. As Chairman, you can continue to be in control (which is usually important to business owners). Wherever possible, you need to make your presence impactful by asking the right questions, encouraging and motivating your successor and management team to carry on your business legacy. As you empower them to make operational decisions, you exercise your "control" card only when absolutely necessary.

## "What's in it for me?"

As Chairman, you continue to have regular meetings and interaction with your successor and management team, who are responsible to keep you informed. Determining and clarifying what expectations you have for each other is important to operational success.

## "What's in it for me and the company?"

Your successor will be empowered and grateful for your support, thus encouraging you to stay involved. Together you can assess if there are other areas where your expertise can continue to be positively impactful (one client said he wanted to be Director of Acquisitions), thus empowering you to stay involved without becoming a liability.

Most importantly, Succession Success™ will be possible for your company. Your dream is to be able to enjoy the business together with your children, feeling the intense joy and pride as you watch your children carry your legacy into the future. You can make this happen by the succession decisions you make.

# 9

# Dealing with Successors

"You're in charge of making
my kid successful!"

# Time Bomb #9

# *Family Members and Your Management Team*

## "BUT DAD SAID I COULD!"

Family business succession can be a touchy issue. "The boss is bringing his kid into the business—this ought to be fun!" said the manager, his tone dripping with sarcasm.

Employees often have this image in mind when they think of the boss's kid: born with a silver spoon in his mouth; gets all the breaks; seen as a great sales person (yet most of the leads were handed to him); comes and goes as he pleases, because he can; will be promoted before he is ready; paid more than anyone else in that job; not held accountable; and potentially poses a threat to their job. No wonder employees cringe when anticipating the arrival of the next generation of the owner's family.

Unfortunately, I see too many examples where the employees are right—the boss's kid is a train wreck waiting to happen. Fortunately, most situations are reversible if caught and addressed early.

When the son or daughter of the owner enters the business, they need to understand they will be under the microscope. Everything they do or don't do will be scrutinized by employees—and this includes wherever they are, not just when they are at the family business. Mistakes will be magnified, and employees will wonder if the boss's kid is the snitch who will be tattling to Daddy.

Social media tends to magnify this problem if one is not careful. The boss's son was supposed to be at a meeting, called in to say he had to miss due to a doctor's appointment, then posted pictures of himself at a social event, which just happened to be at the time he was expected at the business meeting. When confronted, he got indignant, saying, "You're violating my privacy by looking at my social media account." Unfortunately for him, social media is not private.

> When the son or daughter of the owner enters the business, they need to understand they will be under the microscope.

Junior or Sis often enters the business because they are family, not because they are qualified. Without a plan, no criteria have been established for education and experience levels. "We've always assumed my kid was coming into the business, and besides, it's time for her to go to work."

Once they enter the business, expectations are not defined, just assumed. Training is often hit-or-miss, with no specific plan for how to fully prepare for the job of succeeding their parent. In that haphazard situation, it is no wonder at least one daughter or son will enter the family business simply because they are members of the "lucky sperm club." He or she may not be able to get or keep a job at another place of employment. But the thinking goes: "He's our son, and we have to give him a job."

Four sibling members of Generation 2, in their fifties, were arguing as to whether one of their children had qualified to come work in their family business. One of the Generation 2 fathers was adamantly arguing that his son had done what his grandfather (now deceased) had specified was the requirement to enter their family business: two years of work experience. "He worked two years, and now he's qualified to be hired," said the father. "Not exactly," replied the uncle. "Your son worked one year at one company and got fired, and then got fired from the second company. He didn't meet the work experience requirement, and oh, by the way, he has a drug problem!"

I understood where the father was coming from. He deeply cared about his son and was searching desperately for a solution to his son's poor life choices, hoping they could help him if he worked in their family business. Unfortunately, the family business is not going to solve this young man's issues, and instead his entry will create all kinds of family business problems. Can you imagine what the managers of that company were thinking as they contemplated having this son be their responsibility?

With no set criteria for accountability, these family members will often be allowed to work a less structured schedule compared to other employees. COVID created a new paradigm, with so many employees opting to work from home. While this has changed some and differs depending on the industry or company, it created an environment where some business owners' children will take advantage. "But, Dad, I can get more done at home without all the distractions." Clearly, it's harder to hold people accountable when they work from home. In particular, the potential successor children need to be seen and heard, working alongside other employees and managers, building a level of trust and respect.

On top of this is the common occurrence of overpaying the offspring because "we want our child and grandchildren to enjoy a better standard of living." This can definitely affect employee morale and does not ingratiate your child with the employees that someday he or she will be leading.

What are the solutions?

First, establish a Family Business Employment Policy in writing and have family members sign it. This will establish the basis on which each family member will qualify if they come to work in your company. This will help you make the right decisions when confronted by children, in-laws, nephews, nieces, and others who are not qualified.

> Establish a Family Business Employment Policy in writing and have family members sign it.

Second, define your Family Business Employment Expectations Policy in writing and have any family member who comes to work for you sign it. This policy will include whether or not they have to start at the bottom and take the stairs instead of the elevator to the top, what hours and levels of productivity are expected for promotion, training requirements, etc. The more detailed this is, the better. This document should be available to all managers, so everyone knows what you are expecting of family members.

Third, establish a five-year (or more) training curriculum carefully designed to meet the needs of each family member. This curriculum should be developed in concert with key managers willing to participate in a structured mentoring program. Usually, these managers are seasoned professionals who will not be worried about losing their job should they need to hold the boss's child accountable. Key to this idea is that you are looking long-range toward the succession of your company and are preparing your children to be able to take over when the time comes.

Successful business owners are busy people, and it is easy to find excuses for not taking the time to implement the types of initiatives I've been talking about to prepare your children to succeed you. Few people like to think about their own mortality, so it's easy to procrastinate on this seemingly long-range succession planning.

One business owner told me, "What I do is fun; what you do is not fun. So, I'd just as soon avoid it. But if I am going to deal with it, I will need you to push me to address these difficult issues." If this is your sentiment, find someone to push you.

The best situation is to develop a plan when you are still contemplating the arrival of your children in your business and are trying to learn from the mistakes of others—before you start making problems for yourself. Do it right the first time—or be willing to make it right—or you risk damaging your family and your business.

## "EIGHT SECONDS AFTER JUNIOR IS IN CHARGE"

"Eight seconds after Junior is in charge, I'm out of here!" stated the experienced, successful COO of a large real estate development company, expressing his opinion that business with the next generation would be unthinkable. As already mentioned, this view is shared by many managers faced with working with sons and daughters of family business owners who have not held their children to the same standards as they would any other employee. All too often, the child in question is bright and well-educated but has a million excuses.

When employees are scrutinizing your family members, they are looking at three things in particular:

(1) Work Ethic—Are you willing to do any job, not just the glamorous ones? Do you put in the hours just like we have to? Do you come and go as you please because you can get away with it? When you're at work, are you working hard or playing video games? Will you get the job done? Are you willing to come early and stay late if needed?

(2) Attitude—Are you a team player, or is it just about you? Do you care? Are you trying to help us succeed, not just yourself? Do we like you? Can we count on you? Are you coachable?

(3) Talent—Do we believe that you have what it takes to be our leader someday? Are we willing to trust our future to you?

When asked which of these is most important, I get varying responses, but the first two are definitely important. When a successor candidate has a great work ethic and a positive, can-do attitude, the employees will want to help him or her be successful, because they can positively envision this person being their leader someday.

> When a successor candidate has a great work ethic and a positive, can-do attitude, the employees will want to help him or her be successful.

On the other hand, if the successor has the talent but not the work ethic or attitude, they are doomed to failure, and no one will work to help them succeed. For example, consider Johnny Manziel—in 2012, he was the first freshman to win the Heisman Trophy and was later a first-round draft choice in the NFL, yet he played only two seasons and then was out of the league. Talented, no doubt, but plenty of statements questioned his attitude and inconsistency.

How do you handle a child unwilling to do the right things necessary to succeed in your business? The biggest question you need to answer is, "Am I willing to fire my child?" Unless you are, you will be fighting a losing battle as you try to apply accountability.

"The best thing I ever did was to fire my son," exclaimed my business owner client. "Several years later, my son had learned his lessons and demonstrated a changed attitude and willingness to work and be coachable." Today, we are working with this son to help him become the successor he always wanted to be.

When you ask your managers to help develop your child to become a leader in your company, the managers need to know that you have their back. Most of the time, they believe their job is at risk if they hold the boss's kid accountable, so why would they do that? Not only do your managers need to know that you will enforce whatever action they recommend, but your child needs to know that you will stand behind your managers—there can be no ambiguity about that.

The most important thing your child needs to do is earn the respect of those with whom they are working. Without respect, they have nothing. You aren't likely to see this manifest itself in managers leaving you in the short term. After all, they work for you and expect you to be around for a long time. But, when the day comes that you are not here, the productive, effective leaders in your organization may leave as they become easy and attractive targets for your competitors.

**When you ask your managers to help develop your child to become a leader in your company, the managers need to know that you have their back.**

What about the successor know-it-all? While work ethic and attitude are the most important qualities to ingratiate managers to your successor candidate, talent is also important—with one caveat: you must "win the right to be heard," a phrase I learned many years ago when I served on staff with Young Life, a Christian ministry working with high school students.

In a business setting, this advice is extremely important. We've all heard the statement "No one will care how much you know until they know how much you care." That is true, and it is also true that those whose trust and respect you are attempting to earn want you to listen, listen, and listen some more before you speak.

I've had the privilege of working with some very talented successor candidates who have prepared themselves by getting an excellent education and then working in another company, often national in scope, in such industries as banking, investments, or real estate. Their success while working in these other industries was invaluable. It strengthened their confidence to know that they had achieved success on their own, in a company where the employees didn't care who their father was or what he had accomplished.

But, confidence can come across as arrogance, especially if the people with whom you are working in your family business have been there for years.

*"Who does this kid think he is?"*

*"Who is she to tell me how to do my job. I've been here for twenty-five years!"*

Of course, these successor candidates bring a lot to the table and will have ideas that could prove to be invaluable. But no one will listen—and resentment will grow—if they do not take the time to listen first, work hard, be productive at the family business, and build relationships *before* they start telling people what they learned at their previous job.

Remember, your management team wants your successor to succeed, because this ultimately means job security for them. When my partners and I interview managers as a part of our Phase I Succession Analysis, we start by telling them the good news. First, we wouldn't be here if the boss was planning to sell—people hire The Rawls Group because they want a plan to continue the business through the next generation of owners and managers. Second, the boss believes in you, because we asked him to provide us with the names of the managers he trusts and believes in the most to help him plan for succession. We are working to build a plan that will protect and provide for the continuance of the business.

Managers love to see an owner's child who works hard, puts in the hours, comes to work every day with a positive attitude, cares deeply about the success of the company and all the people working in it, and is willing to make sacrifices to earn his way to the top. That's the kind of leader they want to follow. Don't shortcut your child's success—make sure they earn it.

# 10

# Work Life Balance

"All in favor of the expansion project say aye."

# Time Bomb #10

# Family Business vs. Business Family

## WORK-LIFE BALANCE

"I want more work-life balance," exclaimed the forty-four-year-old successor candidate. Having watched her father's generation, who seemed to do nothing but work, she represents the view of most younger generations. Clearly, on paper this appears to be a healthy perspective, but it is a viewpoint with which older generations are usually uncomfortable. In my world and probably yours, this relationship is lived out within a family business, so it affects both your family and your business.

I attended the memorial service for a client of mine with whom I was privileged to work for over twenty years. The church was packed with friends, family, and dignitaries, which spoke loud and clear of the tremendous impact this esteemed business owner and philanthropist had made on the communities in which he had served. His daughter gave a wonderful testimony to her father, espousing his many achievements and proudly commenting on the many people whose lives had been positively impacted by her father's relationship with them. At one point she smiled and said, "There was no work-life balance in our home—every dinner was a family business meeting." I smiled, knowing how true this is for so many of my family business owner clients. Success and impact usually come with a price tag.

One of the reasons why family businesses are such a huge part of the fabric of America, employing a large percentage of the workforce, is because people are often drawn to a workplace where they feel like family. Over and over employees will tell me they love working for the owner because of the family atmosphere. Also true is the concern employees may have working for a family business where they don't share the family name. The inevitable question is "Does my not being a family member create a ceiling for upward mobility?"

**"Family business" is an oxymoron.**

Family businesses are not charities and are in business to make money. Without strong profits, succession will not be possible, and predictably profits may dip during a transition period from generation to generation, especially if this event was premature and unexpected.

Can I maximize profits while still treating my people as family? Is it important to me to find the right balance between family and business?

Meritocracy, accountability, and performance are core values that must be upheld if your business is going to succeed. These values can certainly be manifest in an atmosphere where people are valued and respect is given.

"Family business" is an oxymoron. *Family* is supposed to be about unconditional acceptance ("I love you just because you are my son/daughter"), while *business* is about conditional performance ("What have you done for me lately?"). From my forty-plus years of doing succession planning with family businesses, most family businesses are overbalanced toward *family* or *business.*

When *family* is the predominant focus, decisions are often based on making family members feel good, resulting in promoting too quickly, paying too much, allowing family members to cut corners regarding training, time off, etc. All too often, this approach adversely affects your child's ability to earn respect, which is critical to their success. Regarding non-family, loyalty is highly valued to a fault as employees are sometimes allowed to "retire on the job." Basically, this means the employee is no longer productive, is coasting and just counting the days until he retires.

When *business* is the predominant focus, the needs of the family may be sacrificed "for the good of the business." This often leads to resentment on the part of family members—"All Dad cares about is the business. He never has time for me." This is often the reason why children decide they don't want to be involved in the family business.

At The Rawls Group we like to say, "There is no business gain worth a family loss." You can always make money, but you can't always repair relationships. This might lead you to believe that you should err on the side of being focused on family versus business. But, from a succession vantage point, those business owners who structure the development of their successor children so they must earn their positions are more likely to succeed. This does not have to conflict with family values.

Why does a focus on *family* challenge succession? For one thing, the great American parental dream is to give your children a better life than you had—more education, life experiences, homes, travel, and opportunities. One client told me, "My wife and I struggled to build our business, but our younger children only know the 'good life' and expect first-class everything." It's no wonder your children don't understand when you say you had to sacrifice to build your business. Their perspective on what sacrifice entails is obviously going to be very different from yours.

At the same time, I often hear clients say, "I don't want my kids to have to work as hard as I did." This usually comes from the recognition that you sacrificed family time working in your business, and you don't want this for your children. But unfortunately, most businesses require a significant time commitment to succeed.

**Trying to balance *family* and *business* can be very challenging!**

Trying to balance *family* and *business* can be very challenging! One business owner client told me recently that she sometimes feels overwhelmed trying to stay on top of the demands of her family and business, both of which are extremely important to her. But as demanding as both can be, she and her husband have managed to maintain very healthy relationships with their adult children, while managing a multibillion-dollar business. It can be done.

Unfortunately, there is no easy formula or magic pill that will provide healthy family relationships combined with business success. But those who appear to be successful with *family* and *business* seem to have a few things in common:

- Family time is a priority—protected and regular—even in the midst of overwhelming schedules.
- Family are required to earn their way in the family business. You take the stairs not the elevator to the top.
- A plan for the development of the children working in the business is communicated, so they know what is expected and have a clear path to attaining their long-term objectives.
- Business is communicated regularly via a forum, such as a Family Business Council, where you share your vision,

allowing your children to see the tremendous impact your business is having on your community.

Navigating the potential land mines of *family* and *business* is challenging, but extremely rewarding. Having trusted advisers to help you defuse land mines, clarify issues, and clear the pathway is usually very important to keeping the balance. As I've said many times, "I do a great job talking with someone's else kid—it's a lot more difficult with my own (and they are terrific people)!" Finding the balance that provides business success and family harmony is uncommon but incredibly valuable. As a client once told me, "It means the world to me to have my children involved in our business." That's a goal worth committing to and making work for both your family and your business!

# *Other Family Business Concerns*

## NO SUCCESSORS IN MY FAMILY: WHAT ARE MY OPTIONS?

The dream of having your son or daughter succeed you has not happened. Does this mean you must sell? Maybe yes, maybe no. I've seen this scenario play out many times with a lot of variations, so let's explore your options.

Is your business critical to your financial future? Unfortunately for most family business owners, the answer is yes. Therefore, your succession options may be limited to selling, which I will explore later in this chapter.

The more financially secure you are apart from your business, the more options you will have when the time comes, but that takes years to accomplish, assuming you've committed to building wealth

**Start now to build wealth apart from your business, whether or not you have family successors.**

outside your business. Since this is counterintuitive to the way you grew your business—constantly reinvesting in your business—you will need to adjust your mindset. Start now to build wealth apart from your business, which is important whether or not you have family successors. You will be less likely to "hang on" due to worries that your children will make decisions to negatively impact your financial future. The less you are financially dependent on your business, the more succession options will be available.

> "Can you build a structure that will sustain operations profitably without you?"

What if my children are talented enough, but to date have not chosen to get involved in my business? You're obviously still hopeful this will change, but you feel you're running out of time. You realize your business success is too dependent on your leadership and you're getting tired, or maybe you've had health issues and must face the reality that you may not be able to continue at this pace for much longer.

What if you don't have confidence in your child's/children's ability to run your company after you're gone? They may be actively involved working in your business, but for a variety of reasons they have not demonstrated that they could take over and run your company effectively. What do you do?

The problem is *you don't want to sell*. Your dream of creating a family business succession legacy is still alive, and you are committed to your "business family" represented by the hundreds or thousands of employees with whom you've shed blood, sweat, and tears. Let's face it, you've spent more hours with these people than with your children, and you don't want to tell them they're going to have to work for someone else.

You know there are private equity firms that would love to invest in your company and would pay you top dollar. But, you also know the private equity route means the likely death of your business culture, and that is something extremely important to you. You've always been about the future and operated on a slow sustained growth model, carefully managing debt. Private equity companies want a return on their invested capital—and the sooner, the better.

Getting in bed with a private equity firm would likely mean making changes designed to streamline your operation, with the intent to increase profits quickly. You are fearful the focus would now be on the private equity buyer positioning your company for a quick sale. Preservation of your culture and retention of the people in whom you've invested a lifetime would no longer be important. That is the last thing you want to happen.

The question is, "Can you build a structure that will sustain operations profitably without you?" And for how long? Many companies have leadership who believe they can run the business should something happen to the owner, but can they sustain this for the long haul?

The future of your company without you will require leadership at the operations level, at the board of directors level, and, in some situations, at a trustee level. As is always the case, having the right people is the key. Do you have people who can fulfill these roles to your satisfaction?

Operationally, do you have a non-family manager (or managers) who has historically demonstrated the ability to lead your organization, and is this person of the age that they can be counted on for many years?

Do you have an operating board of directors that is knowledgeable regarding your business and capable of holding the CEO accountable to the values and performance levels necessary to remain competitive in your industry?

Will your family support the leadership team and board of directors? If trustees are involved, do they have the ability to work effectively with your family, the operational team, and the board of directors?

The questions I've posed point directly to the complications involved if there is no capable family member successor and none on the horizon. Unless you are confident you have the right people able to perform in each of the roles described, it is likely this plan will not work, and selling will be your best succession option.

Your problem may be timing—your family member successor is capable, but too young or inexperienced to take over when required. If this is the case, the answer lies in the use of a Succession Bridge®, composed of one or more non-family managers who will lead your company until your family member is ready. Generally, this would include financial incentives to create "golden handcuffs," helping to ensure your Succession Bridge® manager(s) will not depart before your family member successor is ready.

## If Selling Appears to Be My Most Viable Option, What Do I Need to Consider?

Selling is very final, so make sure you know why you're selling. Once you sign the sales documents, your life has changed forever.

I've been involved and worked with many business owners contemplating whether to sell. For many, this is a very emotional issue, as their business has been their life, their focus, and their purpose. They built the business, and it represents their life's work—so moving on is challenging.

For others, it is time to sell, and they are ready to do so. They are tired of the daily grind and want to enjoy the next phase of their life. With no family members involved or capable or willing to take over the leadership, the owner has determined that selling is the prudent step to take.

Timing is often important, as many would-be sellers want to maximize the sales price. Since most businesses are cyclical, it's important to consider the timing in the market to get the best price for your company.

For others, finding the right buyer is more important than price. Most business owners plan to continue living in their community, so the last thing you want to hear is, "It's awful what happened to your wonderful company. The new owners changed everything and ran it into the ground." Taking the time to analyze the culture and organizational fit of your potential buyer can save a lot of seller's remorse.

> **The last thing you want to hear is, "It's awful what happened to your wonderful company. The new owners changed everything and ran it into the ground."**

What are you going to do after you sell? I've often heard, "I'll figure something out." That may be true, but it can be a radical adjustment to move from being the "king of the hill," enjoying the attention of your people and the adrenaline rush of business, to golf and playing cards.

"Sell or not to sell"—that is the question, usually with no simple answers. You invested your life in your business, and you want to end well. Take the time to work through the issues with advisers who have walked through this before. Your legacy is at stake.

## FAMILY BUSINESS IN THE FUTURE

Will family business have a future, or will consolidation and big box stores eliminate family businesses? Will you survive and thrive?

I am not a futurist and I don't pretend to have a crystal ball, but my experience tells me the family business will be alive and well for years to come, especially in the United States. Why? Because the driver of family business is entrepreneurship, and this unique human quality thrives in our country. Depending on your political point of view, we could debate this all day long, but I'm going to hedge my bet based on what I know about human behavior.

I have always been fascinated by entrepreneurs, having spent the last forty-plus years working as a business succession planner with the owners of family-owned businesses. These companies were all started by entrepreneurs, who saw opportunity and committed everything to building their dream. "I didn't know I couldn't do it," remarked the founder of one of the largest portable toilet companies in the U.S.

When I first started in the succession planning business over forty years ago, I was given manufacturing guides, pension guides, and a phone and was told to make one hundred cold calls a day. The requirement was to get a face-to-face meeting with a business owner of a capital intensive, privately owned business with a net worth of $3 million or more. One business, with a net worth of approximately $7 million when I first met with the owner, just sold for over $150 million!

It is amazing to see all the creative ways entrepreneurs have found to make a buck. What an education I received, meeting with business owners of all shapes and sizes, each with a dream and a business that represented his or her life's work.

Entrepreneurs usually want to see their life's work continue. Not surprisingly, most involve family, drawn to this same dream and all it represents in terms of making a difference and building a better life for themselves, their families, and their communities.

Entrepreneurs are amazingly adaptable, adjusting their business model when necessary to meet the demands of the marketplace. My first eleven car dealer clients were all Oldsmobile dealers—not many Oldsmobiles are being sold today except to classic car collectors! But most of those dealers looked for other opportunities and continued their successful family business.

One business owner commented, "I'm spending my money while public companies are being run by people spending other people's money. That's why I can compete." Pride of ownership, combined with the understanding that it is your family's money and reputation on the line, sharpens one's focus, making for clarity in business decision-making.

Consolidation is a reality in so many industries, seemingly eliminating mom-and-pop businesses. To compete, family businesses will have to adjust and, in most cases, grow to a level that keeps them competitive.

Family businesses continue to thrive, despite consolidation. In a McKinsey Global Institute research article by Eduardo Asaf and Acha Leke, published January 3, 2024, they stated, "Family businesses account for nearly 60 percent of private employment in the United States." This article went on to explain why family-owned businesses outperform non-family-owned businesses. The authors stated, "Our research suggests that one important reason for Family-Owned Businesses' higher Total Shareholder Return is superior underlying operational performance." It makes sense to me that when it's my money we're spending, I'm going to be very focused on the results.

I sat in a meeting recently with an eighty-plus-year-old business owner who was challenging his executive team to pay attention to details and not become complacent, even while experiencing record profits. No wonder his company continues to do extremely well—after fifty years in his business, he is not settling for second place!

Not only is this man in his eighties focused, but so are the rest of his family, who believe in their company; are passionate about their mission, vision, and values; and are committed to providing the next generation with the tools to continue their family business legacy.

In my experience, successful family businesses involve owners and their families who are passionate about the impact they are making on their industry and the communities in which they serve. These are the businesses you see sponsoring Little League, AYSO, cancer drives, schools, and a thousand other charitable organizations committed to making a difference in local communities.

Yes, I've seen a lot of consolidation over the past forty years, especially in the auto dealership industry, which makes up a high percentage of my clients. But, for every seller, there seems to be a family-owned dealership group committed to the future of the automotive retail business and to growing and acquiring other auto dealerships.

It is powerfully motivating when your family name is on the building. It keeps you awake at night because you care so much; it gets you up early because you want to do everything possible to see your company succeed. You tend to live and breathe the failures and the successes. But the rewards can be phenomenal, both financially and in your ability to impact the lives of your employees and the people with whom you do business.

That's why I believe the future of family businesses is bright. There are so many opportunities for entrepreneurs and their families to creatively build their companies. Inevitably, entrepreneurs find sons, daughters, and grandchildren drawn to their vision, challenged to continue the family business legacy.

Clearly, family businesses are not for the faint of heart, but when family and business are kept in proper balance, the rewards and impact are priceless.

# HOPE AND ANSWERS

## FIVE THINGS THAT HELP FAMILIES SUCCESSFULLY WORK WELL TOGETHER

"Why do some families succeed from generation to generation while most don't?" expressed the frustrated business owner, clearly looking for answers. "What do we need to do to get it right?"

*Succession* and *Yellowstone* are two recently acclaimed television series featuring highly dysfunctional families, the fictitious Roys and Duttons. Despite their massive dysfunction, both families are tremendously successful. No doubt the dysfunction is why so many people stay glued to their TVs, wondering who's going to blow up next. But dysfunction is not what you want in your real life.

Truth is often stranger than fiction in my world as I work with many highly successful family businesses struggling relationally. "Business would be easy if you didn't have to deal with people" is an expression I've heard many times. And every family is different, so there are no easy answers.

But one thing I do know is that you want your business to be successful *and* your family to be able to enjoy Thanksgiving together. You're not saying, "We're making lots of money, so who cares how we get along."

## Five Things That Help Families Successfully Work Well Together

What can we learn from the many families that are highly successful working together in their family businesses? Let's examine five things

> One thing I do know is that you want your business to be successful and your family to be able to enjoy Thanksgiving together.

I've observed that consistently provide the environment for healthy family relationships creating productive, profitable businesses.

### 1. Family Members Have Earned Respect

They respect each other and have earned respect from managers and employees. This didn't happen by chance. The brass ring wasn't handed to them; instead, they worked hard. Older employees often remark, "I remember when the boss was a kid working for me, putting in the hours and sweating like the rest of us."

Family members bringing an attitude of "What can I do to help you with your job?" are showing respect for those who went before them and are the backbone of any business. This attitude rubs off in the right way, with employees giving their respect because the family earned it.

## What If My Family Members Haven't Earned Respect?

It's never too late—start now. Depending on the ages of family members who suffer from a lack of respect, determine what needs to change and demand change happens. Often this requires the help of a trusted adviser, who will help you examine the behaviors that need to change and begin today to set clear expectations on what needs to happen.

If your son or daughter is twenty-five or younger, there is light at the end of the tunnel, and it will be easier to right the course. But just because your child is fifty doesn't mean change can't happen. Change is a choice, and with a supportive group mentoring via affirmation and kicks in the butt, anyone can change who wants to do so.

Don't expect to see everything change overnight. The expectation of most people around your child (including you) is that nothing is going to change. Don't make this a self-fulfilling prophecy. Celebrate every little win. Every time change happens that you were hoping for, let them know and help them rewrite their script. One step at a time, this is the road to earning respect.

## 2. Commitment to the Family Vision

Without vision, you may be making great time, but you have no idea where you're going. Without vision, companies and families flounder, especially when times get tough. Contrast that with a grandson's comment to me while struggling with a major problem: "My siblings and I will solve this problem because we are committed to continuing our grandfather's legacy of impacting our community and the lives of our employees."

## What If We Don't Have a Clear Vision?

Now is the time to create one. Usually, the owner has a clear vision, but often it has not been communicated effectively to the family and/or leadership team. Unless people are a part of creating the vision, they are not likely to have ownership of your vision.

At The Rawls Group we spend time facilitating the development of a company's vision by involving the key players, including ownership, leadership, and family members active in the business. This is essential to buy-in, creating the motivation to do the hard things that separate your company from the competition.

## 3. Ability to Resolve Conflict

Conflict in relationships is inevitable. The question is, "Do you have the ability to resolve the problem, or are you likely to avoid the issue, hoping it will just go away?" Unfortunately, my partners and I regularly are told stories of decades of unresolved conflict, creating monumental problems for the family and business today.

## What If We Are Lousy at Resolving Conflict?

You're clearly going to need outside help, as this habit is tough to break. Depending on the level of conflict that exists, it may require professional counselors and/or therapists. Fortunately for many, it may be resolved via better understanding of each other's differences—how we communicate (internally or externally), make decisions (intuitively or factually), view the world (through a "people" lens or a "task" lens), and whether we need structure or room to create. At The Rawls Group, when working with clients, we use tools such as ProScan®, designed to help understand each other and untangle the webs that often frustrate and bind people in behavioral patterns that may seem impossible to break.

How is your family inclined to address conflict? Do you avoid issues, attack each other, roll over and just let the other person win? Each person is likely to have tendencies that may or may not be helpful in resolving conflict. Understanding your learned behaviors is the first step toward recognizing how you can change. The Thomas-Kilmann Conflict Mode Instrument (TKI®) is an excellent tool we utilize when helping families break long-standing destructive behaviors preventing them from being able to resolve conflicts.

## 4. Clarity Regarding What Is Expected of Each Other

All too often we assume that we understand what the other person wants from us or that he/she must know what I want because "she's my daughter" or "he's my brother." "We've known each other all our lives, so what do you mean, 'I don't know what she wants from me'?" Sound familiar?

We know intuitively that our family members are different from us and will acknowledge this freely. But, we make assumptions all the time—believing we are clear in what we each want from each other—to our detriment, creating many of the problems that blow up family businesses.

## How Do We Clarify Expectations and Minimize Assumptions?

Clarifying expectations is not the same as defining roles and responsibilities. If you haven't clarified the latter, do it now, because without these being defined, chaos will ensue. Clarifying expectations means defining as specifically as you can, in writing, what you need from the other person to make your relationship work more effectively. For example, "I expect us to meet once a week without interruption to discuss what each of us is doing in our business" or "I expect you to include me in discussions about a particular subject" or "I expect that we will refrain from talking shop when having dinner as a family."

## 5. Commitment to Spending Time Together Discussing Business

This seems so obvious, but it is one of the most violated succession priorities in family businesses. Family businesses are usually very busy places, so owners and their family members are rarely bored. Just the opposite, you are probably scrambling to keep up with all the demands of your business. Everyone wants a piece of the boss, and depending on your leadership style, you may be accommodating too many people or focused on the abundance of tasks and priorities needing your attention.

On many occasions I've heard the next generation complaining, "I can't get time with my father—either he's too busy at work or he's off traveling, and I need his input and help."

## I Know, I Know, but What Do I Need to Do?

Put your children on your calendar weekly. It has been said you can tell what is most important to anyone by looking at their calendar. Make time for the most important people in your life. At work, this includes your successor children.

What is needed is a commitment to structured time scheduled on the calendar and sacredly adhered to. If you want your child to be successful following in your footsteps, he/she needs regular time individually spent with you. This person is your designated successor, whether they are ready or not, so it makes sense that you would isolate time to mentor them. Turn off your phones, shut the door, or leave the office and demonstrate to your child that he/she is important to you.

Some families just play well together in the sandbox. They like each other, enjoy spending time together, and interact well running their family business—without necessarily doing all the things described above, at least consciously. They are the fortunate ones, and since you don't live inside their home or bedroom or boardroom, you may think things are easier for them than may be the case.

For most family business owners, you wish it were easier to integrate your family and business. No matter where you are today, you can find hope and answers. The sooner you start practicing right, the sooner you will be able to make the changes necessary to achieve your family business succession goals and objectives.

## THE FAMILY BUSINESS: IT'S WORTH IT

"I just love my business" is something I hear day after day from the owners of family businesses. Owning your own business is something special, and that is why people continue to risk everything financially to start and build their business.

Why do they do it?

*"I love being my own boss, being in charge, getting to make the final decisions."*

*"I love being able to create a vision and then make that vision become a reality."*

*"I love having my name on the building, knowing I was able to create a plan and build a company that will hopefully last beyond me."*

*"I love that we have been able to give five hundred-plus employees the opportunity to succeed, many of whom are first-generation immigrants."*

*"I love sharing the dream with my family, who are involved side by side with me, building our business."*

*"Our business has created a wonderful life for our family and for the many employees who have shared in our dream."*

*"I love knowing my grandson, who represents Generation 6, is now working in our family business."*

This last statement was made by an obviously proud grandfather and fourth-generation business owner (with whom I've worked for twenty-five years), anticipating the continuance of their family business legacy. He then reminisced with me about his being recruited by his father-in-law, who wanted to see the family business continue. He laughed, remembering his fears when turning over the reins to his son over ten years ago ("What if it doesn't work—I don't want to even think about the negative impact on our family"). Fortunately, we were able to work on the issues creating his concerns, and today his son and son-in-law are doing an amazing job growing the business as partners. Now Generation 6 is on the scene, breaking through the negative attitudes that family businesses can't succeed generation after generation.

> "The best part," this grandfather smiled and said, "is watching my son and his wife and my son-in-law and my daughter all getting along so well as family while doing such a great job with our business."

"The best part," this grandfather smiled and said, "is watching my son and his wife and my son-in-law and my daughter all getting along so well as family while doing such a great job with our business." I replied, "That didn't just happen—you were all willing to do a lot of work to make it happen."

Family businesses are the backbone of the American economy. "The fate of Family-Owned Businesses matters, not only to individual families, but also to society. Globally, FOBs—defined as those whose founders or their descendants hold significant share capital or voting rights—account for more than 50% of GDP," according to the McKinsey Global Institute research article "What Separates Family Owned Businesses from the Rest?" by Eduardo Asaf and Acha Leke, published January 3, 2024.

Clearly, family after family continue to choose going into business for themselves, passing the baton from generation to generation, because it has created a wonderful life for them and the hundreds, thousands, or even millions of people impacted daily by their family business commitment.

Is being in business for yourself risky? Absolutely! Was there risk involved when you said "I do," knowing that over 50 percent of all marriages would end in divorce? Absolutely! Did both stretch you beyond what you thought you were capable of? Absolutely! Hopefully you can say, "It was worth it!"

When speaking at industry meetings, I often begin the presentation by stating, "Everyone, please raise your hand." With all hands in the air, I then say, "This is the answer to the question 'Who comes from a dysfunctional family?' We all do!" This may feel more true for some of us than others, but behind closed doors, we all know the challenges we face in our families.

So, it is no surprise that many of us need help dealing with family issues that impact our business. You're not alone—your situation is not unlike many others. Parents have worried about these same issues for a long time.

In the book of Ecclesiastes, Solomon wrote:

*I hated all the things I had toiled for under the sun, because I must leave them to the one who comes after me. And who knows whether that person will be wise or foolish? Yet they will have control over all the fruit of my toil into which I have poured my effort. . . . For a person may labor with wisdom, knowledge and skill, and then they must leave all they own to another who has not toiled for it. This too is meaningless and a great misfortune.* (Ecclesiastes 2:18-19, 21)

Solomon penned these words three thousand years ago, so your situation is not unique. Parents of all generations have had to address the issues you are facing.

Why is it that you can say with one breath, "I love my business, and I love my family," and with another breath, "I should sell, and they're driving me crazy"?

Being successful in relationships takes work, and being successful in business takes work. Family business combines the good, the bad, and the ugly of each—but the *good* is oh-so *good!* May your family be blessed with many generations of success in your family and your business.

# ABOUT THE AUTHOR

Hugh B. Roberts has worked nationwide for over forty years with family business owners, their families, and management teams to provide solutions enabling family business succession legacies. A partner with The Rawls Group, Hugh has delivered seminars to over seventy automotive 20 Groups, multiple state industry associations, plus ten NADA national conventions. Hugh has a Bachelor of Arts from the University of Colorado, a Masters of Youth Ministry from Fuller Theological Seminary, and is a Certified Financial Planner (CFP) and a Certified Succession Planner (CSP). Hugh is married to Lisa, has two married children and five granddaughters, and resides in Woodland Hills, California.